One Woman's Pilgrimage

Margaret Budd

Speart House Publishing

First published in the United Kingdom in 1998 by the World Methodist
Historical Society (British Section)

This paperback edition published 2017 by Speart House Publishing
Speart House
Morton Spirt
Abbots Morton
Worcestershire WR7 4LY

ISBN: 978-1-911323-04-4

Foreword

In early 1998 I had a telephone call from my Aunt. She had written her memoirs and wanted to know if I would be prepared to pay for them to be published. I was intrigued. Whilst I knew of my Aunt's life as a missionary and later as a Deaconess, I knew little about the life of a missionary. Even the word missionary seemed like a term that more properly belonged in the Victorian era than the twentieth century.

My Aunt had spent most of my early childhood in India, and it wasn't until her return to England in 1968 that I began to know her a little better. She was a colourful, larger than life lady. My memories of her are now limited to small scenes. I recall her coming to stay with my parents and saying that she was going to cook us a proper curry. This was a time before the ingredients needed were available in supermarkets, and the preparation required a tour of all the Indian shops she knew in Birmingham to buy cumin, coriander, turmeric, root ginger and pilau rice. The result was simply the finest curry I have ever tasted. I also recollect taking a lift with her from my parents' house down to Oxford. As she started up her car, she began to sing "Onward Christian Soldiers". I worried that this heralded a heavy religious hour or two in her company. Far from it; it turned out that the hymn's number in the Methodist hymn book had the same digits as the mileage on the car's milometer. The easiest way to calculate the length of her journey: the distance between two hymns.

The first edition of these memoirs was published by the World Methodist Historical Society in return for a small donation. They throw a light on a different world; a world that vanished quickly after the war, never to return. The whole principle of missionary service is now controversial, linked inevitably to colonial rule. To my Aunt it was a normal part of religious life, all set against a backdrop of some of the momentous events of the twentieth century. In this edition I have been able to include some of the correspondence that my Aunt wrote to her sister, Joyce. For these wonderful insights I am indebted to my cousin Helen for agreeing to allow them to be published. They give a more unguarded, personal, and therefore informative view of Margaret's life in China. Whilst going through my Aunt's papers, I discovered some typed notes setting out in detail her return visit to China in 1987. They give Margaret's own historical perspective on the changes in China, and a chance to reflect on her years spent as a missionary. These I have included as a new and final chapter.

The original photographs are now sadly lost. After much consideration I decided to include the copy images from the first edition, on the basis that they were selected by my Aunt as best representing her experiences. I hope readers will forgive their poor quality.

Paul Budd
Abbots Morton
March 2017

Margaret Budd, West Bengal *c*.1965

Contents

Chapter 1: Beginnings

In 1915 there was an outbreak of typhoid fever in the village of St. Buryan in West Penwith near Land's End. The source of drinking water in the village was polluted. The Methodist minister, the Reverend Clifford Caddy, caught the disease and was off work for nearly a year. A young probationer minister, the Reverend Walter Budd, my father, was sent to take his place. Reverend Budd was a Londoner, a Cambridge graduate who had entered the ministry a year earlier and arrived straight from theological college.

On his second Sunday he took the Sunday School Anniversary service at the Wesleyan Methodist Church in Marazion. The soloist was an attractive young lady called Lilian Polglase. It was love at first sight. Unfortunately, they were both already engaged to be married. Breach of promise was considered a serious matter, and their courtship caused a great scandal in Cornwall. The Wesleyan Conference appointed my father to Goldsithney in the Marazion circuit. This meant that he was still close to where my mother lived: at Greatwork, near Ashton, where she taught the piano. However, the news of the scandal reached the headquarters of the Wesleyan Methodist Church and he was moved to Maldon in Essex. He was brought before Conference to answer for his actions. Such was the gravity of the situation that he was in danger of being expelled from the ministry. Good friends in the church spoke for him. He was given two years' extra probation.

He was ordained at the Conference of 1919 and immediately afterwards went down to Cornwall for his wedding. He and my mother were married in the little chapel at Balwest. The wedding breakfast as was at Trewithen Farm, my mother's home. After a brief honeymoon in Torquay they move to Rayleigh in Essex, where I was born on February 2, 1921.

Then began a childhood of moving around. In the Twenties and Thirties Methodist ministers moved every three or four years. In 1922 we moved to Hackney – my sister, Joyce, was born in July that year. She was only two months old when we left Rayleigh. I was two and a half and loved the new manse: a huge building with four storeys. I remember the attic where we used to play for hours on end. The climate in Hackney didn't suit my father and he was very ill with pleurisy and empyema. We visited him in the hospital, where he stayed for weeks on end. In 1925 we moved to the Poole circuit in Dorset. Our church was a large brick built Wesleyan Chapel in Ashley Road in Upper Parkstone. We used to go to Sunday School. There are still a few who remember our time there. My brother, Geoffrey, was born in Parkstone in 1926. I began school while we were there; a private school in Alexandra Road. One day we sang, "All things Bright and Beautiful" at prayers. When I got home my mother asked me to sing it - she still played the piano. I noticed that we had sung another verse at school which wasn't in the Methodist hymn book:

The rich man in his castle,
the poor man at his gate
God made them high and lowly
and ordered their estate.

My mother told me that the Methodists didn't agree with that verse, so we didn't sing it. The next time we had the hymn at school and we came to that verse, I shut my mouth.

Miss Burrows, the headmistress, said, "Margaret Budd, why aren't you singing?"

I replied, "I'm a Methodist and we don't believe in that verse."

That evening Miss Burrows went to see my mother.

In 1929 we moved to Brentford in Middlesex. Our church was on the corner of Windmill Road and Clifden Road. At that time the church was swarming with children and young people. The church had a huge Sunday school with four to five hundred children. During the week the church held all sorts of activities including a drill club. We loved it all. I remember my Sunday school teachers very well and remained friends with them until they died. Brentford had a marvellous free children's library, which I revelled in, as I was a great reader. In it I discovered all the Andrew Lang fairy books, each book with its own colour, and the E Nesbit's books, which I loved, as well as many others.

In the summer holidays my parents took parties of church members on holiday. My sister and I used to go to Cornwall and spend the summer with my mother's sister, Kitty Webb. She and her husband, my uncle John, ran the village store in Carleen. She played the organ in the village chapel and ran the choir. Cornwall was very primitive in those days: water was drawn from wells, and there was no electricity. People cooked and lit their homes with paraffin. Toilets were outhouses at the bottom of the yard. There was no mains sewerage. Aunty Kitty was always busy, so we played wild with the village children. My grandmother died in 1929. The old farmhouse at Trewithen, that had been my mother's home, was sold. As long as my grandmother was alive we had stayed with her. We spent Christmas 1928 at Trewithen and that was our last visit. At Carleen we used to walk two miles or so up a lane to play with the children at Tregonning Farm. The farm was halfway up Tregonning Hill. Mrs Bligh, the farmer's wife, was Uncle John's sister. Mrs Bligh's husband bred Guernsey cows and I was intrigued that the house was full of pictures of pedigree cows but there were no photos of family or relatives. Once a year we went up the hill for a picnic in the Preaching Pit. John Wesley is supposed to have taken services there.

While we were at Brentford my sister Joyce and I were sent to Trinity Hall School in Southport; a boarding school for the daughters of Methodist ministers. We were there from 1932 to 1939, going home for the holidays. In 1933 my parents moved back to

Rayleigh in Essex; and in 1937 it was to Worksop in Nottinghamshire, my father's first superintendency. There's a Trinity Hall corner in the museum at Kingswood School where I learned that, whilst I was at Trinity Hall, fees were £16 a term. The regime at Trinity Hall was quite strict but I don't remember this worrying me at all. We were divided into houses: Cannington, Fernley and Gibson. I was in Cannington. The house colours were green and I wore a green badge. The disciplinary system was a complicated one, based on points lost or gained for the house. We had house meetings every week and had to apologise to the house captain (one of the prefects) if we had lost any points during the preceding week. Order marks were for small peccadilloes, e.g. untidiness. Five order marks were the equivalent of a house point. Three house points were a house mark. House marks were more serious. Worst of all were conduct marks which amounted to ten house points. If you got three of those in a term you were expelled. We got tickets which represented a point for a succession of good marks and could be deducted from the tally of demerits.

On Sundays we were marched to church, resplendent in white dresses and navy coats and hats (Panamas in the summer). After morning service, we went in a crocodile line for a walk on the front at Southport. After lunch we had a letter writing session. We were allowed to buy two pennyworth of sweets to eat on Sunday. At 3 p.m. we had a class which the headmistress took. Senior girls went to the evening service, juniors stayed in. The senior school was in Duke Street, Southport and was the original building founded by John Fernley. The junior school, Wintersdorf Girls School, was a mile away in Trafalgar Road, Birkdale and all the lessons were held there. Every weekday morning, Monday to Saturday, the seniors walked or cycled to Birkdale, arriving at 8.30 when we met our form for gym. Games were played on Wednesday and Saturday afternoons: hockey and netball in the winter, and tennis in the summer. But it was not all work and no play. We had various special interest societies with speakers and activities. We put on plays; I

4

remember our form performing Shakespeare's Henry IV part one. What fun we had getting ready for that. The English Classical Players used to come annually and do a Shakespeare play. I remember their performance of Julius Caesar. Our small stage couldn't cope with all the bodies, so they had to keep drawing the curtains to get rid of them! A Midsummer Night's Dream was a favourite; Bottom and co. were so funny. We used to have wonderful magic lantern shows; I recall a lovely one on the Rose Red city of Petra.

Then there were things going on at Trinity Church that we were invited to. I was one of the favoured few invited to join the choir and we greatly enjoyed the choir outings. A neighbouring Congregational Church used to hold a course of celebrity lectures every winter and our sixth form were allowed to go. We heard all sorts of famous people like Hilaire Belloc, James Agate and Leslie Weatherhead. My music mistress took us to concerts at the Cambridge Hall by the Liverpool Philharmonic Orchestra and started for me a lifelong love of orchestral music.

Academically the school was good. We had a sizeable sixth form for the size of school and most of us went on to university. The staff took a great interest in us all and this continued long after the school closed in 1970. The old girls still congregate for reunions and sing with gusto the school song to the tune "Men of Harlech":

Sing the shield of blue and gold
Sing the name and trust we hold
Sing our motto stern and bold
Plus Ultra! More beyond!

Chapter 2: The Formative Years

I left school in 1939 and all the family went for a holiday in a cottage called Scotland Farm, near Corfe Castle in Dorset. One day, while we were there, we drove into Weymouth to get a newspaper with the Higher School Certificate results. I had passed with a distinction in history. During my last term I had applied for and been offered a place at King's College, London. My result meant that I could take it up. We returned home to Worksop early because the war was imminent. In September, after the outbreak of war, I was informed that the arts section of King's was being evacuated to Bristol and that I would have to find accommodation there. I was fortunate to get lodgings with Donald and Margaret Stoate in Redland, Bristol and lived with them for three years. Sharing the lodging with me was Ivy Belboda, whose father was a West Indian minister in Dominica. Ivy had been in my form at Trinity Hall. Donald Stoate was the circuit steward in the Redland circuit and his wife was a local preacher. She had a great influence on me and was one of the reasons for my call to preach.

Not long after we moved in, the Germans began to bomb Bristol. In the first raid King's library, housed in the Great Hall, was destroyed by fire. For a long time, we had a famine of books. One night a bomb hit the house next door and damaged ours quite badly. The Stoates had a good cellar which we used as a shelter. After the rather spoon-feeding regime at school it took me quite a while to get into the way of study at college. The member of staff that helped me most was the wife of the reader in mediaeval history: Mrs Cronne. She taught me how to use the textbooks and how to write essays. I was pleased to meet her again years later when she was teaching in the external studies Centre at Birmingham University, and was able to thank her.

By this time my parents had moved to Warrington in Lancashire, and when I left King's in 1942 I lived with them and travelled daily to Manchester University for my education year. After this I took a job as a supply teacher for a year with the Warrington education authority. I taught for two terms in a senior boys' school. I was a little innocent and the boys, who came from a slum clearance estate, ran rings around me. They used to ask me all sorts of pointed questions, usually sexual, which I couldn't answer! Fortunately, my mother's brother in Liverpool was at the end of a telephone and could explain things to me. The third term was spent in a Junior and Infants School, which was better. In the meantime, I was busy applying for jobs in grammar schools. I must have sent out dozens of copies of my references. Most of them said they needed experience of secondary school teaching, though how was I to get it if they wouldn't employ me I didn't know. In the end I got a job in the Dixie Grammar School at Market Bosworth in Leicestershire.

While in Worksop, when I was living at home, I used to go to a young people's discussion group on Sunday evenings in the "band room". I only discovered later that this was nothing to do with a brass band. In early Methodism the band was like a smaller version of a class meeting. Mr Bearman, who led the group, encouraged us to try public speaking and leading the meetings. This led to my taking services as an exhorter. When we moved to Warrington I joined a girls' league group at Penketh. My friends there persuaded me to embark on local preachers' studies. I did this by a correspondence course. My tutor was a Mr W.W. Champness who lived in St Agnes, Cornwall. We became great friends although I never actually met him. I was rather a long time on trial as a local preacher; my other studies and beginning my teaching career made things difficult. I was still doing the local preachers' course when I moved to Leicestershire in September 1944. I lodged with a lady in Ibstock called Mrs Bellamy and travelled the five miles to school on the school bus. I was determined to pass my local preachers' exams and began to work hard at it. I soon discovered that I wasn't a very good teacher. I wasn't good at discipline and didn't enjoy the work.

By contrast I loved working in the church. I preached nearly every Sunday, riding my bicycle all around the Ashby-de-la-Zouch circuit. Methodist union still hadn't really happened there, and three circuits overlapped: the ex-primitive Methodist Coalville circuit, the ex-United Methodist Loughborough circuit, and the ex-Wesleyan Ashby circuit. The pattern in these village churches was set to suit the farmers: a 2:30 p.m. afternoon service and a 6 p.m. evening one. In between these services I would be entertained to tea by one of the Methodist families. I remember the names of so many of the villages: Swannington, Griffydam, Shackerstone, Snarestone, Heather, Packington, Whitwick, Moira, Oakthorpe etc. I also ran the Junior Guild at Ibstock and helped with the Wesley Guild. I had never heard of the Wesley Deaconess order or I'm sure I would have offered myself as a candidate.

When I had time, which wasn't much, I struggled with my studies. It was clear to Mr Champness that I hadn't always done my homework. One week, homework included Acts, chapter 8, the story of Philip and the eunuch. He wrote on my paper that Philip's question "Understandeth thou what thou readest?" was a pun in both Greek and Latin. "Intellegis quae legis?" He said that to get the idea of the pun in English you would say, "are you taking in what you are giving out?" the pun working because the eunuch would be reading out loud. Mr Champness wrote, "that's the question I want to ask you this week." I have never forgotten this. It was a sorrow to me that, when I could have met him before I went overseas, he had just died.

During all this time my faith had been deepening. Scripture lessons at our Methodist school were not very inspiring. We studied the Bible in sections. I only realised its wholeness when, in 1942, I

8

read Fosdick's book A Guide to Understanding the Bible. The move to Warrington was a step forward. Whilst there my close relationship with the Girls' League made a big difference. Their notes for group discussion taught me a lot. While I lived in Leicestershire I became the District Girls' League Vice President, visiting the various branches in the district. I was a delegate to Girls' League Easter conferences, one in Weston-super-Mare in 1943 and the other at Wentworth School, Boscombe in 1946. At the same time, I was feeling more and more the call to serve as a missionary overseas. I began to attend missionary conferences run by the Methodist Missionary Society. All these were a source of great inspiration and I met some very interesting people. The Reverend Harold Rattenbury, who had served in China for over thirty years, and who was later to become President of the Methodist Conference, used to chair the missionary conferences. Among the speakers were: Dr T.F. Davey, medical superintendent of the Leper Colony and General Hospital at Uzuakoli, Nigeria; Reverend Harold Beales, for Bible study; Alan Birtwistle, Barbara Simpson hot from war-torn China, and many others. My local preacher studies were giving me a good grounding in biblical and theological knowledge. Whilst at Manchester University, during my education year, I went to a course of lectures by Dr T.W. Manson, the Professor of Biblical Criticism, about the connection of the Old Testament with the New. He was a well-known biblical scholar and this was a great privilege. In 1945 I was received as a fully accredited local preacher.

Chapter 3: Training For Mission

In the spring of 1946 I went before the candidate's committee of the Methodist missionary society for assessment as to my suitability as a missionary. I was accepted and sent to Kingsmead College for a year, beginning that autumn. Kingsmead was one of the Selly Oak colleges founded by Sir Edward Cadbury, and sponsored by the Methodist Church. Courses of study on theology, old and new Testament, church and mission history were run by the Central Board who employed well-qualified staff as lecturers and teachers. The only snag was that Kingsmead was run like a girls' boarding school, which we resented.

The winter of 1946 to 47 was very cold. The whole country was short of everything. We were still rationed and there was very little fuel – I used to wake up to an icy bedroom almost with icicles on my nose and my towel and flannel frozen. Nevertheless, it was a good year and I especially enjoyed the international community. In the winter term the Selly Oak colleges put on "1066 and all that" in aid of displaced persons in Europe. Kingsmead performed two of the scenes: Henry VIII and his six wives, I was Anne of Cleves "with a face like a Flanders mare", and the Oliver Cromwell scene, "he's got a wart on the end of his nose". It was all great fun. Towards the end of that term we spotted crocuses in the snow under the Cedar tree and knew that spring was coming. There were about thirty women students at Kingsmead and most of us were appointed to China. The general opinion was that we could begin again where we left off; how wrong they were. By June 1947 I knew that my district in China was to be Ningpo, a port in East China to the south of Shanghai. I began to correspond with the Coombs sisters, Doris and Kathleen, who were to be my colleagues.

In July my father came in his car. He picked me and my belongings up and took me home, which was near Rotherham where he was superintendent minister. The Methodists in the Circuit all wanted to help me. The ladies were busy making dresses for me and cutting up parachutes to make underwear. A hardware merchant insisted on making me two steel trunks and made them far too big. They weighed a ton when crated. We went up to London for the annual valedictory service at the Kingsway Hall, in Holborn, and then took part in a local valedictory at our own church, Talbot Lane. By the end of September, I was all ready to go.

At sea, wartime regulations were still in operation. The ships commandeered by the Navy had not been returned to the shipping companies like P&O and Anchor Line. In the event it was November before I heard that I had a place on a boat, the good ship Lancashire, a Bibby Line boat hired by P&O. On November 20th my father and I travelled by train to Liverpool and spent the night at my uncle Tom's home in Bootle.

November 21st was the day I sailed and also the day Princess Elizabeth married Prince Philip. It was a miserable November day, drizzling and dark. There were five of us new Methodist missionaries en route to China: Edna Whewell, Margaret Barnard and Margaret Gregory were being posted to Yunnan in south-west China, Rene Lowther to Hunnan and myself to Ningpo. My father and other's relations stood on the quay but out of earshot – they were not allowed on board. It was a relief to us all when we actually sailed. The Lancashire had about a thousand troops on board going to join the army of occupation in Japan – they slept in bunks in the hold and there was room for about eighty passengers. Some of the passengers were wives with their children, going to Japan to join their husbands. There were also about twelve missionaries and a few folk travelling to Singapore or Hong Kong.

There was a popular song of the time "Slow boat to China" and I reckon the Lancashire was the original of that song! It took us six weeks to reach Hong Kong. There was nothing much arranged to keep passengers and children amused – no hosts or hostesses, no swimming pool. The passengers had to organise themselves. The Captain asked the five of us to do an evening service: religion was classed as an entertainment. Two of the soldiers' wives took hymn practice on a Saturday. Their knowledge of hymns was nil and the Captain only knew hymns like "Onward Christian Soldiers"! When it was realised that the army children were noisy and out of control and preventing the ships personnel, especially the night staff, from getting their sleep, the Commanding Officer started broadcasting messages over the relay: "Children will be quiet between 1 o'clock and 5, if not they will have to leave the ship at our next port". The frightened mothers asked us to run a school for their children on weekdays. We took turns on board and also held a Sunday school on Sunday mornings. When it got close to Christmas we were asked to organise a carol singing session for the troops and a Christmas party for the children. Amongst the other missionaries on board were: Mrs McGavin (and her son) whose husband ran the Bible Society in Shanghai, Miss Lloyd and Miss McGrath of the Japan Evangelistic Board returning to Japan and Mrs Jensen, a Danish Pentecostal lady. Mrs Jensen had the most extraordinary ideas. She said to me one day, "We know the end of the world is coming because of meat rationing". I replied, "Do we? How do you know?" "It's all in the Bible," she replied, and then referred me to a verse in Revelation: "When you shall see the mark of the beast then shall the end come". And she said the mark of the beast was when the butcher crossed out your coupons for the week's ration! She disapproved of Margaret Barnard being an agriculturalist and told her she should be taking the gospels to the Chinese and not crop seeds. Margaret had a lot of seeds in her baggage which she planned to experiment with in Yunnan.

There was a storm blowing in the Irish Sea when we set sail. I had never heard of seasickness pills although Kwells were on the market. We all slept well and got up before the second sitting of breakfast, but before I got to the table I was seasick. Someone dosed me with Kwells, but it was too late. I had a wretched three days as the storm didn't abate until we were through the Bay of Biscay and nearly into the Mediterranean. After that I bought some Kwells for myself and kept myself under for the rest of the voyage. I have never been a good sailor, but I learned to control it. We stopped in the Grand Harbour at Valetta in Malta – I was still feeling ill, so didn't go ashore. Our next stop was Port Said by which time I felt well enough to enjoy it. The Gooly Gooly man came on board and pleased the children with his conjuring – baby chicks all over the place. After that we stopped at Aden and enjoyed the shops. I often wonder where all those shopkeepers went to. The boat also stopped at Colombo. To our joy we were met by the Reverend Basil Jackson, a Methodist missionary working in Colombo, and also Miss Elizabeth Roper, who had been head of the Junior School at Trinity Hall. She was now headmistress of the Princess of Wales School for girls near Mount Lavinia in Ceylon. Miss Roper took charge of Edna Whewell and myself, while Mr Jackson took the others. We had a wonderful day at the school, and had lunch with Miss Roper who showed us the sites of Mount Lavinia.

The best of all was Singapore - where we stayed for two days. The second day was a Sunday and we went to evening service at the Cathedral. It was a great thrill to meet the Reverend Joshua Ban-it Chiu who had been at King's College and whom I had known in the International Society and Student Christian Movement. He later became the Bishop of Singapore and now lives in Verwood with his English wife.

After the service we took a taxi and asked for Gate 4, the Docks. We were a bit puzzled by the route the driver took until he drew up with the squeal of brakes and announced "Number Four Gate, the Dogs". He'd brought us to the greyhound track! How we laughed – but he didn't charge us for his mistake. We got back to the ship and we were soon on the high seas again. Christmas Day was a few days later. The five of us, together with Miss Lloyd and

Miss McGrath, went carol singing around the ship. We came on an open space where there was a cage-like affair. Inside were about twelve Japanese soldiers. We had heard there had been some taken on board at Singapore. They were going to Hong Kong to be tried because of their cruelty to British men on the Death Railway in Malaya. Miss Lloyd and Miss McGrath produced their Japanese hymnbook and sang a carol in Japanese. They all bowed to us as they recognised their language. Later in the day the stewardess brought a note from one of the Japanese soldiers to the two missionaries. He wrote his thanks for the carols and said that he was a Christian, as were two of the others. Our bit of fellowship meant a lot to them. In the afternoon we took the children's party and helped the staff feed them.

We expected to arrive in Hong Kong on Boxing Day, but in the middle of the morning the ship did an about turn and started going back the way we had come! We discovered later that we were heading into a typhoon and the captain was taking avoiding action. It took us another two days to reach Hong Kong. We were met by the Reverend Donald Childe, who had been interned in Canton during the war. He took us to the Soldiers and Sailors home where we were to stay. The home was run by the Reverend J. E. Sandbach, a missionary who had also suffered internment. I stayed at the home until New Year's Eve when I embarked on a decommissioned American troop ship called the General Meigs. They were holding a New Year's party at the Soldiers and Sailors home, so I was put on board early. Until after midnight I was about the only person on board. I think all the rest were at parties and I felt really deserted. At about 11.30 Mrs McGavin and her son Murray arrived and was I glad to see them! The ship sailed about 3 a.m. and we realised that it was empty of ballast and we tossed up and down like a cork on the water. Everybody was seasick. We were one day and two nights on board and arrived at Shanghai early in the morning on January 2. In the customs shed, as we waited for my luggage to be vetted, my colleague Kathleen Coombs, who had come to meet me, said,

"I hope we won't be too long as we're going to see the film of the Royal wedding this afternoon!"

After a few days in Shanghai, Kathleen and I went down to the quay to catch the boat to Ningpo. There were two ships which went to Ningpo and back, one in the daytime and the other overnight. We embarked in the evening, slipped on board and arrived early morning at Ningpo. A whole contingent of Chinese friends came on board to welcome me. We couldn't talk to each other but we could smile and Doris and Kathleen translated for me. I had arrived.

Afterwards, at the house where we were having breakfast, I said, "I'm so looking forward to being settled." Doris said, "what makes you think you'll be settled? There's a Civil War on and the communists are going to win it." I knew nothing of the real situation in China. I remembered a conversation I had with Miss MacGrath on board ship one evening. I had made a similar remark about looking forward to being settled, and she replied, "China is in the middle of a Civil War and you don't know how long you'll be able to stay." I protested that I believed God had called me to give my life to China. She said, "do you think that God will alter the course of history just for you?" I couldn't answer that one and she said, "remember this, whether you are in China for two months or two years you will have obeyed God's will. God will be with you."

As it turned out I had just under two years in Ningpo – an unforgettable time. The mission compound was over a hundred years old. There were four houses – my colleagues Doris and Kathleen Coombs had the first, I was allocated the second, the Reverend Jack Gedye lived in the third and one was in ruins. Next door to us was a primary school run by the Mission and next to that a small private clinic and hospital run by Dr Samuel Wu. Dr Wu was a Methodist and was our doctor. His married sister, Lily, and her two children were living there and she was my first Chinese teacher. Her husband was the Reverend Marcus Chem who was a leader in the China Christian Council.

My very first day in Ningpo I was taken to see Lily Wu and introduced to her. I was to go to her every day after breakfast for an hour's lesson. Then we went to the house of an eighty-year-old pastor – Pastor Hsi – who was to give me my Chinese name. Doris wrote my name "Margaret Budd", on a piece of paper and Pastor Hsi studied it for a while and then wrote some Chinese characters on the paper. He announced that my name was Bah Mai Ga – Bah means "white" and Mai Ga means "beautiful mustard"! That evening Doris and Kathleen had invited other missionary friends to come for a party and to meet me. There was Sylvia Colantonio from a Pentecostal Mission, Dr and Mrs Thomas and a nurse, Billie, (whose surname escapes me) from the American Baptist Mission, Mr and Mrs Smith from the American Presbyterian Mission and with them a new young couple, Earl and Berneita Harvey and their baby daughter, and Miss Esther Gauss, Doris's senior colleague at the Girls' High School. They were all people I was to get to know very well in the time I was there.

The next morning, I went to Lily Wu for my first Chinese lesson. In the course of conversation, I said something complimentary about Madame Chiang Kai-shek. Lily nearly bit my head off. She told me that Madame and her family's name was mud in China. Her famous brothers, H H Kung and T V Soong, were busy lining their pockets and so was Madame Chiang Kai-shek. Chiang's son was running nightclubs in Shanghai. I was very upset. It was so different from what I had heard in Britain. When I got home I taxed Jack and the Coombs: "Were the missionaries telling lies when they spoke so approvingly of the Nationalist government?" Jack explained that most of the missionaries only remembered the early days of the Chiang government – after that they were either sent home or into internment camps. Kathleen had been at home in Plymouth while Jack and Doris were both in internment camps in Shanghai. Jack had been the London Missionary Society Superintendent before the war and was interned in Hankow. After being released at the end of the Japanese war, he remembered the bitter disappointment at the demoralised state of the Nationalist troops as they marched in to Hankow. The long period in unoccupied China had been too much for them. Jack said it was very sad because they had been so good at the beginning in the 1930s. Now their troops had all-American equipment. By contrast, the communists had to make do and mend but were winning all the victories in the North. It was only a matter of time before they took over China. The Chiang government were busy moving all their assets to Taiwan. Every time the communists took a city in the north, inflation took a jump as the people's confidence plummeted even further.

Chapter 4: Beginning in Ningpo

My first task was to learn Chinese. At that time Ningpo people used a dialect of Mandarin Chinese and this was what I had to learn. We used the same Mandarin script but pronounced it differently. For example, the character for "men" was pronounced "nying" in Ningpoese and in Mandarin it was "zung". I was amazed to find that Chinese has almost no grammar, any word can be any part of speech. There are no tenses - you can only know from the context whether the sentence is past, present or future. The biggest job was learning the characters and how to write them. Characters were grouped under radicals - the radical formed part of the character but had nothing to do with the sound! Although there were thousands of characters, about two thousand formed a working vocabulary. I enjoyed learning Chinese and playing around with the characters. I was very lucky to have Lily Wu as my first teacher - she was excellent and a real scholar.

About my third week in China I had a visitor. He was Dr Hu, the pillar of the church on the other side of the river from our houses. It was a new church whose members were made up mainly of recent converts. They had acquired a harmonium and he had heard that I was musical. Would I like to become their organist? He thought it would help me to feel more useful while I was learning the language. I felt he was right and Doris agreed. So for the rest of my time in China every Sunday morning after breakfast I cycled across the city to Kong Tong church. It was a dwelling house located in a busy street. The Biblewoman, Mrs Ghew, lived downstairs. Upstairs the wooden walls between the rooms had been dismantled to make one big room. The harmonium was by the pulpit, so that

I faced the congregation. The programme was as follows:

9 to 9:30 a.m.	Hymn practice. I had to teach the members a new hymn every Sunday.
9.30 to 10.00	Prayer meeting
10.00 to 12.30	Morning service

Most of the people spent all day at the church and brought their lunch with them. I had mine with the Biblewoman and her young grandson downstairs.

1:30 p.m.	Two or three girls from Doris's school arrived and took Sunday school children for an hour
2.30	There was a session on Christian endeavour. They had a handbook with themes for each week which members of the congregation who could read would lead.
3.30	A preacher would arrive to take the afternoon service. If it was a minister this was followed by Holy Communion or Baptisms, infant and adult.

I would play the hymns for the whole programme and cycle home exhausted, about 5:30 or 6.00 p.m.

This link with a local church became very valuable to me. I got to know the people well. They were puzzled by me at first - why couldn't I understand what they were saying? They shouted at me because they thought I was deaf. So one Sunday morning Dr Hu put up a blackboard and called me out. He explained to the people that I had newly come from a land far across the sea, that I wasn't deaf, and that I was studying Chinese. Then he passed me a piece of chalk and in simple Chinese he asked me to write some Chinese characters on the board which I did. Then he gave me a Bible and got me to read part of Chapter 1 of St John's Gospel, which he knew I was reading with Lily Wu. He told the people to pray for me and to speak slowly to me and if I could reply they would praise the Lord. After that time, they were so friendly and helpful. They were amazed to hear of a country that didn't understand Chinese!

One Sunday morning I was a bit late and forgot to lock my bicycle which I left just inside the door downstairs. Later I remembered and ran down to lock it, but it had gone! It wasn't mine, it belonged to Kathleen Coombs. When I got back to the harmonium, the Biblewoman could see I was upset and asked me what was the matter. I told her about the bicycle and she rushed down to see for herself. When she returned, she told Dr Hu who in turn disappeared. He had gone to report the theft to the police. In the meantime, I carried on playing. After lunch Dr Hu organised a prayer meeting to pray about the bicycle! Actually we never saw it again. But I was amazed at how concerned they all were about my loss.

As I couldn't always understand the sermons and facing the congregation as I did, I would observe their faces with interest. In February 1948 it was Chinese New Year and one woman convert had persuaded her husband to come to church with her. She came in beaming from ear to ear. Behind her came her husband scowling away, with his hat on and a cigarette in his mouth. He sat down on the ladies' side and a steward moved him in with the men, took his hat off and got him to stub out his cigarette. He looked so fed up that I thought he would never stay. But he did! As the day wore on, he mellowed and responded to the friendliness shown him. The following Sunday he was there again and later in the year he was baptised and became a member of the church. Nearly forty years later when I revisited Ningpo I met him again and he remembered me!

Amongst those people attending were a number of blind people. One in particular, a Mr Chang, used to sing his heart out. In China in those days the blind people usually became beggars and lived on the streets in groups. I asked Dr Hu about the blind members. He told me that when Kong Tong Church first opened three or four years earlier they became concerned that as Christians they ought to do something to help the city. They prayed about it and someone suggested that they help to rehabilitate blind beggars. They went in groups of two or three to meet the beggars at night in their sleeping groups and talked to them. Would they like to learn a trade? If so, the church people would help; apprentice them to somebody and raise money to set them up in business. About eighteen beggars said they would like help in this way and were duly apprenticed to Christians who had a trade: noodle making, rope making, cooking, etcetera. Some returned to the streets and they ended up with about twelve, eight of whom converted to Christianity and became members at the church. Chang, the singer, was a cook and had a shop where people could eat or buy the things he made. He was married and had two children. Chang was another member I met forty years later. I was amazed at this story, further proof of the practical outworkings of Chinese Christians. Dr Hu told me that they were continuing this social work and thinking about new fields of service.

I was asked to play for the women's meeting which met on a Tuesday. One Tuesday I arrived to find all the women coming out of the Church with Dr Hu. He explained that one member was ill and they were going to have the meeting at her house. So off we all went and eventually arrived at a building divided into tenements. The lady in question had two rooms upstairs. While the doctor was attending to his patient, some women went to the kitchen and put rice on to cook, others started cleaning the other room. They collected her dirty linen into a bundle to take away and wash for her. They gave her a bed bath and changed her clothes. Then we all sat around her bed and held the meeting with prayers and hymn singing. Dr Hu gave a short Bible talk. Then they brought her some rice and vegetables to eat and gave her a cup of green tea. Then they washed up. We said goodbye and left. I discovered that they often did this for members who were ill, as they did for sick neighbours and other people who needed help. That church really cared for people. I developed a great admiration for the Chinese Christians.

While all this was going on I was getting to know the city of Ningpo (now called Ningbo) the city of the Peaceful Wave. It hadn't always been peaceful. It was one of the centres of the Tai Ping Rebellion. There was a foreign graveyard just along the riverbank from us where there was a memorial to the British soldiers who served under General Gordon and who had died in the campaign. Sadly, there were also many graves of missionaries who had died of tropical diseases like malaria and dysentery and sad little graves of their dead children. Ningpo was one of the five treaty ports handed over after the Opium War, through which foreigners were allowed to trade. There was a British Customs house and, until the Second World War, there had been quite a large foreign concession population, mainly British and American. It was also the city where Hudson Taylor began his mission work and where the China Inland Mission was founded in the 1860s.

There were a number of mission centres besides ours. Our mission was founded by one of the more Free-Church Methodist groups – the United Methodist Free Churches - which later joined with the Bible Christians and others in the United Methodist Church in 1907. Just across the fields from us was the Bethel Mission, a Pentecostal group with several missionaries. The American Baptists on the other side of the city had a large hospital called Hwa Mei. Dr and Mrs Thomas were in charge and the nurse we called Billie. The American Presbyterians were also active. Mr and Mrs Smith were their senior missionaries with two new colleagues, Earl and Berneita Harvey, and their baby daughter. The Anglicans also had a compound with a priest and his wife, Reverend and Mrs Duddington, and Mollie Churchill, a missionary who did teaching and pastoral work. We were all members of the Ningpo Missionary Fellowship and met at the Smiths once a week for a prayer meeting. The Christian Churches in the city were: the Centennial Church, the new building put up by the Anglicans when they celebrated their centenary; Fu Ji Church which was Presbyterian; and three Methodist churches – Kai Ming (which means Open Door) in the centre, Kong Tong in the East and Poh-dong just on the north of the river.

Letter written by Margaret from Ningpo to her sister Joyce, detailing her time there:

Methodist Compound
39 Bah So Lu
Ningpo
Chekiang
East China

Wednesday, February 25

Dear Joyce,

    I'm sorry I haven't written before to thank you for your Christmas card and birthday letter. The time flies just as quickly out here as it does at home. Anyway, thank you very much. I don't know how many of my letters home you've seen – I meant to suggest that mummy send them on to you but she said in her last letter that she'd send them to Aunty Kitty. They get the most detail in their letters – I'm busy trying to catch up with my correspondence and as you can imagine find it rather trying writing the same news lots of times! Presently I'll do a general letter for Maggie Booth to send to less intimate circles.

    I'm glad you got the news about our day in Colombo and Elizabeth Roper. I have some photos which I'll send you when I have the prints. I'll enclose what I've got – one or two I sent to mummy. How'd you like Roper's artistic curls? I was quite annoyed to think that Ma and Pa got the Singapore letter twice over considering the effort I expended!

    I'm taking it that they won't see this one, so let's hope they don't happen to be in London when it arrives! The point is this – although at the moment Ningpo is a very peaceful spot, and it's a job to realise all the goings-on elsewhere, the fact must be faced that one never knows what may happen. Only last week there was a communist landing in Shanghai – it was defeated and was only a small one – but if Shanghai was cut off our mail would be held up. So if by any chance my letters ceased for a while and the parents start worrying, tell them it doesn't mean that Ningpo is affected. Ships from Shanghai or airmail could easily be affected. I thought there was no need to tell Ma and Pa this now or they would worry unnecessarily and there is no probability of it happening at all. You can't prophesy about the situation in China now – it's quite unpredictable.

In view of the political situation I feel you should read the enclosed classic item of news as it appeared in our paper the day before yesterday! I'm sure you will appreciate it!

At the moment I'm sitting in the sun and feeling that the winter is really over. Actually I've been much warmer this year than I was last year - we had plenty of wood and have really kept nice and warm. Chinese New Year was about a fortnight ago and they usually reckon spring begins about then. It's like Christmas, spring cleaning and Guy Fawkes all rolled into one. We went out to lots of feasts. I'm liking Chinese food very much but, if I don't go carefully, I get awful indigestion! Last Sunday we went to one which turned out to be the nicest I've had so far. We had ten dishes! They included the famous shark's fins, turtles, fish, chicken, goose, pork served with hot bread rolls and finishing up with bowls of rice and in the centre – eggs, meatballs and vegetables. All negotiated with chopsticks and a spoon!

Everyone has been on holiday over the New Year so my Chinese lessons have been suspended for a fortnight. I started again this week with a test! Nancy Gedye stayed with us for ten days and proved a very entertaining companion. Mr Gedye is her brother. She is a perfect scream. Kit Cundall popped in for breakfast last Tuesday on her way from Shanghai to Wenchow. She sent you her love – she is engaged and hopes to get married in the summer – so her stay in Wenchow was a very short one. Her husband to be is a missionary in Hupeh.

Talking of marriage hoping to hear of your engagement soon! Geoff's already done it I hear. I shall be interested to hear all the information from your end particularly when Pat arrives. I hope the arrangement works well and that she and mummy fit in alright. I hope Geoff is soon enough for daddy to get him into college next autumn. I'm glad you're sharing

24

Faith's flat – you'll be much better than at Bauds. Mummy says Peggy has gone back to Cornwall – because of her father's illness I suppose.

You say I've got all the news and you haven't any! But this isn't so – I want to hear all the gossip from your end – how you're getting on with Emily and anything you don't think the parents would think of telling me.

Chinese is a funny language quite different from any European one. The grammar is so different – there are no tenses to the verbs, you have to stick in another word to show if it's past or future. If you want to ask for hot water you don't say "have you got some hot water?" But literally "hot water have?" 熱 水 有 哪 些 (just to show my cleverness! You pronounce it Nyih sur yiu vueh?) I'm beginning to pick up phrases like "Feh yaw Kah chi" – don't be polite and "Ti chi nyih" – the weather is cold and "ching ching chmoh" – please eat etc. It's great fun learning them. I can count too, right up to the millions, and I even understand when Vong Me (one of the servants) told me that two people were too much for one commode!

I get on very well with everyone here. Doris and Kathleen are good sorts – Doris being the most approachable. I think Kathleen feels the Chinese like Doris better than her. She likes everything well organised and things as they should be and shall never be able to organise the Chinese. They will make rules but they simply can't keep them. Doris is more easy-going and was here during the war and got to know the folk more closely than Kathleen did. Doris was interned and Kathleen was at home all the war but there was a long period when missionaries were still doing their work even after Pearl Harbour and it was then that Doris got so close to the Chinese Christians. Mr Gedye is very nice – he is a great tease. He is loaned from Hupeh at present but is hoping to stay here. We have asked for more staff which we need very badly. It looks as though we may get some of the North China people descending on us before long. It would be nice to have a family here.

Life is really very ordinary and not at all spectacular. It's surprising how quickly one gets used to seeing things Chinese. I'm quite accustomed to rickshaws and coolies and to seeing shop assistants eating their meals *in the shops in full view of the street; and to bowing to people instead of shaking hands. There's one thing the Chinese do know - how to keep themselves warm. They don't have fires inside their houses except the charcoal braziers which keep their feet warm. Then they add one padded gown to another until they get really fat! They wear knitted Chinese trousers which come down to their ankles – the gowns come down well below the knee so you can't see much of them. The braziers are a good investment. I have one myself – if you wear Chinese cloth shoes you can rest your feet on them. They are made of brass and they stay hot for ages. You put red hot charcoal in the bottom and cover up with ashes.*

I am going to take a primary class for English this term, so am wondering how I'll get on with my limited vocabulary. There are only twenty of them and if they misbehave I can turn them out altogether! The school is next to the compound and the kids make a terrific row all the time. I'm sure I don't know what they get up to. Doris says they have ten minutes' rest after each lesson!

I shall have to close down this letter or else I shall be overweight. Also I've got to lead prayer meetings at Missionary Association this afternoon (it's Thursday now! I stopped to play tennis yesterday) and I want to have another look at my "utterance"!

Give my love to Faith and anyone you meet who knows me (that's a bit rash I think)

Lots of love,

Margaret.

P.S. we have applied for three new missionaries, a ministerial probationer, a teacher and an experienced missionary – Mr Gedye says it is to allow me to make my choice!

The people I knew best of course were the people I lived and worked with - Doris and Kathleen Coombs and the Reverend Jack Gedye. About a year after my arrival, Reverend J. Hooper, known as Peter, arrived. Kathleen went home when her mother died in April or May 1948. Doris was only with me at weekends as she was on the staff at the Riverside Girls' High School; her colleague there was an elderly American missionary, Miss Esther Gauss. Doris had been in China for twenty-one years - she and Jack had spent the war in different internment camps in Shanghai. When my parents asked me what Doris was like, I wrote back that she was like Friday's Child, "loving and giving". Although we were in different houses we all ate together and were looked after by two women – Yiling Sao and Vong Me. We had a gardener called Adong.

I had been brought up as a Wesleyan minister's daughter and now for the first time I was in a different set-up. Doris, Kathleen and Peter were ex-Bible Christians. Jack, like me, was an ex-Wesleyan. Later on in India I found myself in an ex-Wesleyan District where the emphasis had been on founding institutions - schools, colleges, hospitals etc. The United Methodist Church went in for sharing institutions and not going it alone. We had a share in Hwa Mei Hospital, and in the Girls' and Boys' High Schools, but their main thrust was training the ministry and building up people of God. When the communists arrived, they at once took over all the institutions but the People of God went on growing.

About two hundred miles south was the ex-United Methodist District of Wenchow. The Church in Wenchow, like the church in Ningpo, was growing fast. The Methodist Missionary Society wanted us to join up. But there were no direct communications between Ningpo and Wenchow - to get to Wenchow we had to go to Shanghai first - another two hundred miles north. Also the languages were different and they couldn't understand each other. In January 1948 the District Synod met in Ningpo and representatives from Wenchow were supposed to be with us. In the event the communications were so bad that they didn't arrive until Synod was over. The Missionary Society was advised that joining up was impossible. During Synod we had to appoint a new Chairman of the District. During the Japanese occupation when the missionaries were interned, the Chinese ministers worked loyally for the church on very low pay. As a result, most of them contracted tuberculosis and all needed long-term medical treatment while I

27

was there. The retiring Chairman, Dzing Sing Ming, was so ill with tuberculosis that he couldn't continue. With great regret the Synod had to accept his resignation and appointed the Reverend Eo Tong Zing in his place. As for me, I was to continue learning Chinese and gain experience to prepare for a lay training job, teaching new Christians about Christian life and faith.

Letter from Margaret to her sister Joyce in the Spring of 1948:

Methodist compound,
39 Bah So Lu
Ningpo
Chekiang
East China

Thursday, April 7

Dear Joyce,

Two things from you have arrived in the last two days – one is the letter with the two MRA (Moral Rearmament) booklets and the other is the first two magazines that you're subscribing for. Thank you very much – I like your choice of magazine. I don't know if you have written the letter you said you were going to on February 19th – but it hasn't come.

Having written to you twice in fairly quick succession I seem to have let far too much time go before writing again. Sorry! My intention was to try and write regularly.

I hear Ma and Pa's trip to London was cancelled – they were looking forward to it too. Anyway, by the time you get this you will have been home for Easter – which also means you will have read all my letters and got all my news!

The other week Jack brought two Chinese naval officers home from church with him – we had an ex-American destroyer escort here for about two months. One of them was trained at Devonport and of course Doris was very interested. The other one was a Methodist from Wuchang. They've been here two or three times and on Monday came to play tennis

– Doris and Peter were on holiday. We invited them to come again on Saturday but the ship sailed yesterday. (We had been shown around it a fortnight ago by the captain who'd had training in Germany and America). We went outside to watch them go past yesterday afternoon and they all began to wave to us – first the captain and then Mr Yu and Mr Ching, the two officers, and finally half the crew. It was quite exciting!

As you'll have heard, I had a fortnight in the country with one of our Biblewomen, Miss Chang. She's given me a great time. You'd like her – she's got a great sense of humour. I've been to all sorts of places – the people all want to give you tea and something to eat until you nearly burst. On Easter Monday I'm going down to Ziang Saeu and Shih Pu with Jack and Mr Eo, our chairman. We have to spend the night on a dirty little coastal boat but Jack says there aren't any bugs at this time of year!

It's Thursday evening and Jack, Peter and I usually sit by the fire at night. Peter always prepares his lessons – he's muttering over them now. He likes to put the whole English lesson into Chinese in case the boys catch him out – he'll be hairless soon! Jack is muttering the wedding service in Chinese – he's marrying a couple on Saturday – I am playing "here comes the bride!" By the way if you could get hold of cheap copies of the Lohengrin and Mendelssohn wedding marches I'd be very grateful. They are an indispensable part of the missionaries' equipment! I can always get the money to you through the mission house.

Which reminds me – Mrs Chen, my old Chinese teacher, wants the next six months bookclub books and I want to give them to her. So I filled in the coupon and I am writing to Miss Porter to tell her to let you have the money when you apply for it. Mrs Chen also wants Trevelyan's Social History; which was the October choice – you can get back numbers okay I think. For the money write to Miss H.M. Porter, 25, Marylebone Road, NW1. I hope you don't mind me bothering you about this. I'll write again when I know you haven't seen my home letters!

Lots of love

Margaret

P.S. do try and get Ma and Pa (not forgetting yourself) to have a photo taken

During Synod the members from all over the district were staying in Ningpo, some with family or friends, but many actually in our compound. The women members stayed with us and I got to make many new friends. The three remaining houses in the Methodist compound were just over a hundred years old. Professor Soothill, who became the first Professor of Chinese at Cambridge University, lived in one of them. He was the father of Lady Hosie, who was born there and married the British consul in Shanghai. She was the author of a number of popular books on China. In our garden was an ancient Gingko tree, a tree from the ancient past, a prehistoric tree, in fact primeval. In this country it's known as the Maidenhair Tree. It has male and female trees. We also had a beautiful creeper on the front of our houses called a Trumpet Vine with brilliant flame-coloured flowers. Our compound was right on the bank of the River Yong on a road called White Sand Road – Bah So Lu. On my balcony I could watch the junks and barges going up and down the river. It was very quiet and peaceful.

Letter written by Margaret to her sister Joyce, Spring 1948:

Methodist compound,
39 Bah So Lu,
Ningpo,
Chekiang
East China

Monday, May 17

Dear Joyce,

Thank you very much for your letter – I'm glad you got mine all right. From all accounts you had quite a good time at Easter. According to Mummy, Daddy and Frank get on well together. I hear you and he are having a holiday together. I shall look forward to hearing your more "concrete" news!

I'm most impressed by your prowess as a housekeeper. I expect you've heard from mummy that I'm housekeeper here too – but I don't have to do any cooking – I'd like to learn, but don't seem to find time. Tonight you will be at home having your dresses made. You'll be finding Mrs Gilbert a real artist at dressmaking.

Yes, I saw Jean Sellers wedding announcement and was highly amused that she'd pulled it off. It isn't any of the three young men she was "on" with at Manchester. What an outlandish name too! I haven't seen Winifred Moor's yet – that recorder hasn't arrived yet. No – we haven't got our probationers! There'll be one bachelor to eighteen unmarried women at Kuling – Mr Gedye is afraid the competition will be too keen for me!

The Chinese had their first "so-called" general election at the end of January and their first National Assembly in March. Up to then only one party was recognised – the Kuomingtang. But in order to make the election "general" the Kuomingtang allotted some seats to each other party. Unfortunately, not enough of the members of each small party were elected to fulfil the agreement. Then there was a row – so Chiang Kai-shek asked certain Kuomingtang members to give up their seats to small party members. They refused and were declared unelected and went and sat in the Assembly Hall and hunger struck. However, the police removed them and the assembly was able to meet. Then the delegates began to attack the government. Kuomingtang had a "splendid" program drawn up and the delegates refused to keep to it. In fact, they very healthily said what they thought and let off a lot of steam and everyone felt better. I regret to say that most thinking Christians don't like Chiang's party. I don't think they're very fair to him – he's been hedged in by people who have more power than he had and who wanted their own way. They have a very corrupt officialdom and the local government is thoroughly inefficient. The classical example of the government departments ways occurred last week – a boat at Shanghai had a thousand more people on board than it should have had and their luggage. The port officials fined them and they paid the fine and sailed! Why they don't have more ships sunk than they do is a mystery to me! There were two missionaries on board that ship and they thought their last hour had come. Actually, the bulk of the people can't really take part in an election because they're illiterate.

Having been home you'll have read all my letters and all about my country trip and probably have seen the photos I sent home. I gather that in the country the communists are more imminent – people just don't mention them to each other. It isn't wise. You can see workmen building forts all round Ningpo - that doesn't mean anything particular. On the north the communists have been persecuting the Christians and particularly the Catholics. I realise now that Christian communism is a very different thing from political communism which is completely anti-Christian. The Christians don't all realise what's coming to them if the communists come – but some of them do. We should just have to clear out if they began to approach here – but there isn't any sign of it yet. If the main armies got into this area they would be joined by lots of malcontents and bandits in the hills around here.

Well, now after all that, I'll give you some sidelights of life in Ningpo. You get my main news from home and will probably be more interested in these tales.

We haven't any plumbing here – and use commodes et cetera. Chinese ones are rather low and Mr Gedye who is very tall has a Chinese bucket. One of our servants – Vong Me – is a real scream and always acts what she says. She met Mr Scott one morning and imitated Mr Gedye sitting on the commode just to show how awkward it was!

Last week Mr Scott came back from a visit to the hospital behind us, with an invitation to supper with Dr Wu (Wu's are a big Christian family – one of them is my language teacher) so at 7.30 we sallied forth and found Mrs Wu waiting at the gate. She looked so surprised to see us and said that we were invited for the next night not that one. Mr Scott must have made a mistake. So Mr Scott apologised profusely and we rushed home to get some supper. Mr Gedye pushed his head through the hatch and said: "Hao Ky'uoh" and surprised the servants taking a bath in the kitchen! What we really think happened is that Dr Wu didn't tell his wife about the invitation until it was too late to prepare. So in order to save face they said we'd made a mistake. The next night we all went in grand style and had a slap up do, and everyone felt fine.

We have a cat with four kittens and I'm having a great time bringing *them up. They are awfully sweet. Mother insisted on carrying them all upstairs after they were born – when I tried to bring them down we had an awful time chasing kittens as she tried to take them up again. The kittens were shrieking and it was terrific. So I gave in and they're still up there. Now they are a month old it's time that they came down and ran around – so I'll have to try again.*

I don't think I'd better embark on another page now or you will never get this. I'm off to my Chinese lesson now and then to a wedding feast and all.

So goodbye for the time,
much love,
Margaret

Chapter 5: Interlude in Kuling

In April 1948 I was allowed to go on holiday to Kuling, a mountain resort in central China, about three hundred miles west of Ningpo. Usually new missionaries didn't get a holiday when they had only just arrived but Jack and Doris wanted me to have the chance to go as it almost certainly wouldn't be possible by 1949. How right they were. As soon as I was paid at the beginning of April, I was taken to the money market and changed my money into sixty silver dollars. It made my luggage rather heavy but was the only way to finance myself while I was away. I embarked on the steamer for Shanghai – I had a bunk in a cabin for ladies and slept very well. Gordon Ward, our Mission treasurer met me and took me to his house in Route Culty, which used to be in the French Concession in Shanghai. Also on her way to Kuling was Kit Cundall from Wenchow. She was going to marry the Reverend Desmond Gilliland while at Kuling. We were going to travel up the Yangtze River on a river steamer. We had to wait two days to embark because of a typhoon which lashed the city. Then at last we were on board. As well as Chinese passengers there were a number of missionaries from various societies, and also some Russians. There was a big colony of White Russians; refugees who had fled from Central Asia at the time of the Russian Revolution. They all had stateless passports and were very worried about the prospective communist takeover.

It was an interesting trip up the River. There had been flooding and many of the houses were partially submerged. There was a new American missionary on board who was a source of amusement to Kit and me with some of the things she said. One day she said to us, "do the Chinese always build their houses underwater?". The food was Chinese but very eatable. However, at every meal she longed for something American. We sailed past Nanjing where now a bridge crosses the river and also through an area where communist pirates were active. Then at last we reached the town of Jojiang where we disembarked. Kit's fiancé was there to meet us. We got a taxi to the foot of the hill where a crowd of coolies with sedan chairs shouted for our custom. Nowadays there is a motor road up the hill, but then you either walked or were carried in a sedan chair. The views were magnificent as we climbed. I was taken to bungalow 24B where several missionaries were staying, including some who had been at Kingsmead with me. Kit was staying with her parents who were missionaries in the Hupeh District. Kuling was a beautiful mountain resort with lots of lovely picnic spots, waterfalls and pools where we could swim. When I revisited China in 1987, I didn't get to Kuling, but saw lots of picture postcards of its beauty. It's now a place where many Chinese families go for holidays and is called Lushan. While I was there an American Presbyterian couple, Dr and Mrs March, arrived bringing Earl and Beneita Harvey and their little girl, who had nearly died of dysentery.

The big event that year was Kit and Desmond's wedding in the Union Church. Kit was carried to the church in a decorated sedan chair and looked gorgeous. I was the organist and had to play an American organ with a leak in the bellows. The register signing took hours and I had to repeat my repertoire four times, much to the amusement of the congregation. The reception took place at the Cundalls' bungalow. It was a day to remember – the bridesmaids' dresses were made by Mrs Doris Russell who had been a court dressmaker before she married J Arthur Russell.

We used to vie with each other about how much we could get when we changed our silver dollars at the money shops in the bazaar. The exchange rate fluctuated all the time but was mainly upwards. I decided to buy myself a tea set. Jojiang was a centre for pottery making and there were many China shops in Kuling. I got one in the traditional butterfly pattern for thirty-six million Chinese dollars which equalled about thirty shillings at the time. I still have it. On the Sunday after my purchase Generalissimo and Madame Chiang Kai-shek came to church. They came late and went early so no one got a chance to talk to them. Madame Chiang Kai-Shek's father had been a Methodist Missionary. Generalissimo Chiang Kai-Shek was baptised in his wife's Methodist Church soon after they married. We heard that they were trying to halt the galloping inflation by issuing a new currency. It didn't work – the new currency inflated worse than the old; no one had any faith in the Nationalist government any more. We were glad we had our silver dollars!

Letter from Margaret to her sister Joyce, Summer 1948:

Lot 24
4 Yang Road,
Kuling,
KI

Monday, August 9

Dear Joyce,

This is just a short note to say a belated "many happy returns of the day". I'm sorry I've not written before but I came away without your new address. Now I've decided not to wait till I get back but to send the hanky via home.

Pat tells me she's going to share your flat – I shall be interested to hear your angle on the happy couple. How's Frank? I hope you had a good holiday in Wales.

We just had tremendous excitement. We heard that Generalissimo and Madame Chiang were coming up – they have a bungalow here. So we dashed off down to the gap to wait for them – after over an hour they arrived in their chairs. We were quite close to them and got a special smile from Madame. All the people clapped them – they don't cheer in China. Madame is very good looking – the Generalissimo is looking old. He must have plenty to worry him. I don't know how long they'll be staying – not long, I expect, with the situation as it is.

I won't write any more now as it's late. We're pretty busy with rehearsals for a concert we're giving next Monday and I thought if I didn't send the hanky off now, it never would go.

Goodbye and much love,
Margaret

PS Will someone be kind enough to tell me how Pat spells her surname? I invent it every time I write.

PPS I'll write again when I get to Ningpo and tell you more news

My time in Kuling was drawing to a close. The Marches and the Harveys were planning to leave soon and Jack had written that I was to travel with them. We were no doubt seeing the final days of the old Kuling. The different valleys were occupied by different groups – the White Russians had their own valley and so did the British. The Americans had their own section. The Chiang Kai-shek's had their own holiday Palace. There was also a boarding school for missionaries' children which had moved down from Tsuingtao, a seaside resort in the north when the communists got too near. Now their days in Kuling were soon to be numbered.

I decided to walk down the hill and got coolies to carry my luggage. Mr March also walked, but Mrs March gave up halfway and took a sedan chair. The Harveys used sedan chairs. At Jojiang we went to the railway station and took the train to Hanzhou. Travelling by train in China was quite a treat. Each coach had an attendant who provided each passenger with a mug and a little packet of green tea leaves. He boiled a kettle and came around at intervals topping up your tea! In 1987 on my visit back they still did that.

We had three days in Hanzhou. The Marches used to work there – he had been principal of the Presbyterians University – so had many friends. One of them treated us to an outing on the famous

West Lake. We had a boat to ourselves and went to Imperial Island for a marvellous meal in a hotel there. It made a real contrast to the Nurses' home at the Anglican hospital where we were staying and where life was fairly spartan.

We caught a bus to Ningpo on the third day. They were repairing the bridge across the river which the Japanese had damaged. As we crossed we looked out of the window right down to the river below. It was quite a dangerous crossing but the Chinese didn't mind taking risks. We reached Ningpo mid-afternoon and I was home by teatime. It had been a great expedition. I had met most of the missionaries who worked in central China in the Hupeh and Hunan districts and had seen a very beautiful part of China and had the chance to see Hanzhou which is very famous.

Letter written by Margaret to her sister Joyce, Summer 1948:

As from Methodist compound
39 Bah So Lu
Ningpo
Chekiang
China

Sunday, August 22nd

Dear Joyce,

Having received a letter from you I feel I should write a proper letter in return. I hope you've received the hanky okay – I'd like to have bought a better one but funds wouldn't permit. I've bought several odd bits of embroidery to send to various folk for Christmas presents etc. I'm sending a cloth to mummy by Mr Scott who's sailing in October.

Today the weather has been just frightful, terrific squalls of rain the like of which you never see in England. It just buckets down. The place has been shrouded in clouds all day and you can't see anything. But we had some very good weather previously, so we can't complain. We are at least cool. No – there aren't any communists here! If there were, we wouldn't be here! They are mostly in North China, but pushing down towards the Yangtze. The Generalissimo and Madame Chiang have been up but they don't show themselves much.

I'm sorry the air letter made you finish off just when you were getting warmed up. I should be very grateful if you could write more often. Mummy and daddy – although they write every week – don't seem to give me a connected picture of what's happening. For instance, I'm really rather at sea about Geoff and Pat – one minute he's going to college and the next he's not, with no real link between the two. Then I'd like to know what you read in the English papers about China. I'd be interested to get cuttings about that. And I never hear what's going on in politics either. If you wrote more often I would too of course in reply to yours. How about it?

I'm glad you had a good time at Llangollen. When I was at a summer school at Shrewsbury two years ago, we went on a trip to find Llangollen and drove all around the horseshoe pass. I thought it seemed rather a nice little place. The pass was beautiful but we thought the charabanc was going to break down!

Last Monday our mission gave a concert in the auditorium here. It was a good show – though I say it, a mixture of musical items, burlesques and two one act plays. The audience was a receptive one and saw most of the jokes. Rene Lowther wrote a burlesque on Snow White and the seven dwarves in rhyming couplets. The witch was a very senior missionary; Snow White was a sweet new missionary and Prince Charming was an American doctor straight from Yale. I was the Prince! It went over like hot cakes and was the hit of the evening. We brought in a lot of topical jokes – the theme being that the witch was trying to stop Snow White marrying as so many of them had gone "down the drain".

Which leads me onto Kit's wedding. She was well and truly married on August 6. Remind me to send you a snap next time I write, as I can't enclose one in this. We all had a great time dressing up for the occasion. She'd asked me to play the organ – its bellows leaked and it was awful hard work. My repertoire (which was all I could play on it) was limited and *they were in the vestry much longer than I expected. I went round and round my repertoire much to the amusement of all!*

She is now Mrs Gilliland, wife of Reverend Desmond Gilliland who hails from Ireland and is stationed at Wusueh near Hankow. As for her views on Faith – she doesn't seem to have known her very intimately. We talked about Faith in Shanghai and she really doesn't know a lot about her.

Recently Ma and Pa have been very reticent about Geoff and Pat, so I've been wondering. They do seem to be getting about – driving at night and dashing down to Cornwall and back again. I hope they don't wear themselves out. Has the basic ration been given back? Otherwise how do they do it? That's another thing – how's rationing going on? has anything come off the ration?

Goodbye
lots of love
Margaret.

Amid her Chinese friends at Chingri in 1948

When I arrived home I found we were having a visit from the Reverend Donald Childe. He was to take over from the Reverend

Harold Rattenbury at the Mission House in London and so was visiting districts he hadn't seen, before he went on leave. His visit gave us the chance to raise a number of issues that we had with the Missionary Society. It was obvious that the Mission Boards at home didn't understand the situation in China. We knew the communists were going to win the Civil War. The Mission Boards kept writing to us about not losing our nerve and so on! Gordon Ward in Shanghai was fed up because he wasn't allowed to join the United Mission treasury which all the other British missions belonged to, so that he had to work alone. We hoped that Donald would be more reasonable.

Chapter 6: Out and About

My colleagues, both Chinese and English, were very good to me. We all realised that the future of China was in question and they gave me every opportunity to go out and about and to see as much of China as I possibly could. My first outing was with Kathleen Coombs to a village called Chi-ji. There was a new church there founded by a Christian doctor, Dr. Yiang, from Ningpo. He was a convert and he and his wife felt called by God to practise in and around Chi-ji. He lived there for several years and founded three or four new churches, making a large number of converts. Unfortunately, several months before our visit he died of typhoid fever and his wife returned to Ningpo. Kathleen and I stayed in his house in Chi-ji which was now the home of two Biblewomen who were nurturing the new churches.

His surgery was still there just as he had left it. We had a most interesting visit. The Christians came from miles around for a meeting the first day. The Biblewomen told us they were studying the book of Leviticus together! Kathleen decided to use the story of the Sower. We sang hymns - the Biblewomen sang a line at a time and we sang it after them. Hardly any of the people knew how to read. Kathleen explained to them that I was newly come from England and that I didn't know much Chinese yet – they were all so friendly and loving to me, I felt a real sense of fellowship with them. On our way home we visited the other churches and stayed at the home of a lovely lady – a Mrs Chang whose husband had been a catechist assisting Dr Yiang and who had also died in the typhoid outbreak. We travelled home as we had come, on the launch. There was a string of boats pulled by a motorboat at the front. Beggars moved from boat to boat begging and singing for alms. It was springtime and the fields were yellow with sesame flowers. Pear trees were all in white blossom.

On my next outing I stayed for three weeks with a lady called Miss Wang. She was really like a deaconess and had the same training as the ministers at the Nanjing Theological Seminary. I had a wonderful time with her – she took me to all her village congregations and helped me prepare short addresses in Chinese to give at the services. One church we went to were very worried about a young bride who had married a year earlier into a village family. Her in-laws were angry with her because she hadn't started a baby and she had become very depressed. Everybody thought she was possessed by evil spirits. For a time, the Christians boarded her at the church and she was constantly prayed for. I found that it was common to bring invalids to the church – many cures were talked about as a result of this practice. Healing was by the whole congregation working together and not by individual healers. While the girl was at the church she was all right but when the family took her back she relapsed. We asked the Christians why they thought the healing hadn't lasted. They replied with reference to the story in Mark 2 about the paralysed man whose four friends brought him to Jesus. The faith of his friends helped to heal him. When the girl was with her unsympathetic family her own faith wasn't strong enough and the family had stopped allowing the Christian friends to visit. Miss Wang and I managed to visit her and prayed with her, but she was deeply depressed. I never heard what happened to her, but suppose she was sent home.

On my last day with Miss Wang we visited a wealthy Christian widow. She lived in a large house with a few friends and servants. Miss Wang took a number of Christians with her and led a Quiet Day – though nothing the Chinese did was ever quiet! The widow provided us with a marvellous Chinese meal at her own expense. When it was time to go, she lent us a boat and called on two boys to take us home. One used the towrope and the other the big oar and rudder at the end of the boat. The widow had eiderdowns laid down for us to sit on. It soon became obvious that the boys were not expert boatmen! The towrope became tangled when one of them tried to throw it under a bridge. We had to wait while he untangled it. Once we were on the canal, the boats we passed became tangled up in our towrope and he knocked hats off people who were walking on the tow path. Miss Wang and I laughed till we cried – it was so funny. The next morning, I was early at the canal to catch a boat home to Ningpo. Miss Wang came with me as she had a meeting to go to. Like me she was worried about what would happen to the widow when the communists came. The widow was a considerable landowner. We all knew the writing was on the wall as far as the result of the Civil War was concerned. But the fighting was still north of the Yangtze River. In the south we still had a little time.

Letter by Margaret to her sister Joyce, New Year 1949:

Ningpo

Monday, January 31

Dear Joyce,

Thank you very much for the Christmas card and calendar which arrived a few days ago. Sea mail takes two months at least – we have had some in six weeks but not often. Most of our Christmas mail sent by sea had been sent too late, and arrived at least a fortnight after Christmas. Not that it matters, but I know you'd prefer it to be on time, so I thought I'd tell. The stuff that arrived in time was sent in October!

Thanks a lot for offering to subscribe to a magazine for me. It'll be very welcome. Doris and I thought we'd like a woman's magazine and plumped for Women and Home. Then in my last parcel of magazines from home there were three of these labelled "grammar school". If this is to be regular, then maybe you'd like to choose another one. To be truthful I've forgotten the names of most them! I've asked Ma and Pa to tell you if the grammar school magazine is to be a regular.

I got your birthday card too – thank you! I'm wondering if I'll get any more from anyone else.

I'm sorry about the Mah Jong rules but it's quite an impossibility for me to find out. The Christians won't have anything to do with it as the Chinese who play gamble so heavily on it. They sit up all night and lose fortunes, if they've got them to lose! So if I was found enquiring about the rules I should be considered very questionable. I'll tell Pat this myself when I write.

with love,
Margaret

My next visit was back to Chi-ji in February 1949. Since my first visit they had built themselves a church. At Synod they were told they could apply for a grant from England, but said, "no, we'll go ahead ourselves." And they had. People gave their labour for free. They were given timber by a Christian firm in Ningpo. The boat delivered it to a little port about three miles away and everyone who could walk went to collect it, carrying it the three miles to the site. Now the church was about to be opened. They invited the whole district. About five hundred people came and they fed everybody for several days. There was a church, a courtyard and a new house for the Biblewoman and visitors. I remember being put to bed on a rather rickety camp-bed. I fell asleep almost immediately, at which point the room was empty, but when I awoke I was in a sea of sleeping women dossed down on the floor. I couldn't see how I was to get up, especially when they all started kneeling and saying their prayers. I was surrounded by praying women, so I joined them. It was a thrilling occasion. I was told that among that throng only about a dozen had been Christians before 1942. About 11 o'clock we all queued up outside the church and sang choruses.

"Glory to his name! Glory to his name!
The precious blood of Jesus has cleansed my heart.
Glory to His Home!"

Mrs Yiang cut the ribbon and we all sang our way inside. I was seated at a harmonium. The first hymn was given out – a long one and when I started playing I realised the harmonium been wrongly reconstructed with the bellows working backwards. I struggled to the end of the hymn and wondered how I was going to manage! We then prayed – the Chairman leading and then everybody praying their own prayers out loud. When the prayer finished I opened my eyes and to my amazement there was another instrument in front of me. Someone had noticed my struggles and during the prayer had changed the harmoniums over. Talk about an answer to a maiden's prayer!

They had invited a special preacher from Shanghai – he was very excitable and taught us to sing a verse from Ephesians 5 verse 17 which he took as his text: "Do not be fools but learn what the will of God is." We sang it about a dozen times until we knew it. He had twenty-two points to his sermon and after each point we sang it three or four times, with the result that I have never forgotten it and can still sing it after fifty years. It was a good way of teaching illiterate people. Their church opening for me was a wonderful opportunity to meet a cross section of the membership of the Ningpo district. I was very impressed by the quality of the Christians. Many of them were very poor but generous to a fault.

Before the war brought things to a close, I still had one more wonderful outing. Mr Eo, the District Chairman was planning to visit the Southern Circuits of the Ningpo District. He invited me to join his party because he was anxious for me to see as much as possible before the communists arrived. In the group were the Chairman, Reverend Eo Tong-Zing, Reverend Jack Gedye, Mr Ching Ti-on the District treasurer, and myself. To give me female companionship he also asked along a young Chinese lady, who was training as a deaconess. We set out in the middle of April 1949, just a week or so before the communists crossed the Yangtze River, on a Chinese junk which took us about thirty miles along the coast to a natural harbour where we disembarked on to a small boat which took us to a small village where there was a church. They fed us and put us up for the night.

The next morning after breakfast we all went to the church for a service. The church was built at the foot of a hill and on the hill was a flag flying with a red cross on it. They flew it whenever they had a service. We were now in the Ning Veng Circuit and their Minister joined us for the duration of our stay in his circuit. During the morning we passed through several villages where there were recently built churches. The villagers were all out in the fields planting rice, so we just saw the buildings. It was fascinating seeing all the work going on in the fields – they had ways of pumping water from the streams into the fields. There were flowers blooming all over the place including wild yellow lupins, and all over the hills pink and yellow azaleas. Soon we crossed over into Ziang Sare circuit – Ziang Sare means "Elephant Mountain". As we approached the town of Ziang Sare itself, a procession came out to meet us – the primary school band plus a group of men, women and children all singing hymns and songs of welcome. I felt like royalty marching into the town. The street was lined with people all showing their welcome. Jack and I were a nine-day wonder. Because of the Japanese occupation and the war, it was about ten years since any white missionaries had been seen in that area. We were allocated hosts and went home with them for a meal and to get ready for an evening service later. I shall never forget that service; every window and door was crowded with curious faces and the church was full to overflowing. Mr Eo had instructed me some weeks before to prepare some short addresses with my Chinese teacher, as he planned for me to speak at some of the meetings. I was included at this service with Mr Eo himself, who had been the Minister in Ziang Sare before he became chairman, Jack Gedye and Mr Ching Ti-on. It went on for hours with loud praying and singing of hymns. Jack said to me the next day, "the church in this district has become truly indigenous". I felt all along that though they liked having a few missionaries around, they didn't really need us. They were quite capable of running their own affairs.

We spent three days in and around Ziang Sare, visiting the various village churches and taking meetings. Families vied with each other to invite us to a feast and on the morning we were leaving we found ourselves eating a Chinese feast for breakfast, which was a bit much for our digestive systems. Then we went our way, up hill and down dale. I lost count of the churches we visited and the services we took. The country was absolutely beautiful and full of interest. One night we spent at a village called Du Ts where the villagers had blasted a flat place on a hilltop and on which they had built a church and pastor's house. We held an evening service there and the people came in from the fields after working all day. Their enthusiasm was infectious. When it was time to go home they produced paper lanterns tied to sticks and lit them, going singing on their way. We watched dozens of little lights bobbing into the distance as they went. It was unforgettable.

The next morning, we were off again. This time the path ran along the seashore until we reached a coastal town called Jah Chi. On the beaches were dozens of fishing boats obviously ready to set off. I was told there were shoals of fish about to arrive – the fishermen were watching for them and would sail as soon as they were spotted. This town had evidently been founded by North China pirates about three hundred years ago. We received a great welcome and their hospitality was generous to a fault. After a meal I was put to bed in a four-poster bed and fell asleep almost immediately.

The next morning after breakfast and a time of prayer we were taken to visit the local government leaders of the town. They invited us to a feast that evening and we were treated as honoured guests. Then we were taken around nearby villages and churches, all of which had been recently built. In some of them we led prayers and talked to the people. Most of them also came to the main service held in the Jah Chi church that evening. Once again the church was packed to the doors with crowds looking in from outside. I gave one of my little addresses which Mr Eo expanded on!

When we left the next day, the boats were all gone from the beach – the fish shoal had arrived. Our next port of call was a place called Shing Jaw – New Bridge. The minister here was called Dzang Ts-Fong. He had contracted tuberculosis during the war and for a time completely lost his voice, but he was now getting it back. We only had one night there, but it was special. Mr Dzang was a spiritually minded man and we had a wonderful time of fellowship after the service that evening. We all knew it was only a matter of time before the communists arrived and we prayed about it. I remember thinking, this church and Ningpo will survive – they have what it takes. In 1987 when I revisited Ningpo I met Mr Dzang again and many others who had suffered a lot but remained faithful. He was still playing a leadership role.

Next day being Sunday, we attended worship in the Shing Jaw church, led by Mr Dzang and Mr Eo, and then we were off again. We were still near the coast and could see the fishing boats busy out at sea. The water was boiling with large fish. We were soon out of the Ziang Sare circuit and into the Shih Pu circuit. This was to be our last port of call. En route we came to a large village with a church, where they were in the middle of the service. We went in and joined them. We soon realised that they were all praying hard about the future. News had been heard on the radio that the communist armies had crossed the Yangtze River and were on their way south. When we reached the town of Shih Pu that evening our first enquiry was when the next boat would go to Ningpo as we realised we must get back as soon as possible. However, there was to be no boat for two days, so we had to be patient. The Superintendent Minister, the Reverend Wong Me-Dong, was delighted. "You'll have time for a proper visit", he said, and so we did. Shih Pu is a beautiful place with a large harbour. We were taken on a boat trip around the harbour, calling in at some of the many islands surrounding it. We attended at least six or seven meetings in the two days we were there. We visited the schools and shared in a Sports Day. I gave the prizes!

Two days later, at midnight, we embarked on a very crowded coastal steamer. We managed to find room to sit on the deck. When I got up to look at something, the captain shouted at me to sit down in case the ship tipped over! We realised the boat was dangerously overloaded and prayed hard for our safety. Our prayers were answered. It was a beautiful moonlit night and the sea was as calm as a millpond. As we sailed along, the hundreds of islands making up the Chusan Archipelago were silhouetted in the moonlight. We arrived at Ching Hai at the mouth of the Uong River at dawn and sailed the ten miles to Ningpo – an experience I shall never forget. I often think of all those people that I met and wonder what happened to them. I do know that the Reverend Wong Me-Dong died in prison in 1951; imprisoned because he owned some land. On our visit to Ningpo in 1987 I learned that the church in Ziang Sare and Shih Pu was flourishing and that Du Ts was bursting at the seams with young people.

A few days later we heard that the communists had taken Shanghai. They then bypassed Ningpo and took Wenchow. Chiang Kai-shek's troops were refugeeing through Ningpo – the river was full of boats. The Nationalists were taking lorries and tanks to pieces and taking with them whatever they could on the ships to Taiwan. They were also looting wherever they could and the people were more afraid of them than they were of the communists. Then at last on May 24, 1949 the communist troops arrived in Ningpo and occupied the city. As they came in the Nationalists went out – we learned later that it was all arranged beforehand. All the firing was into the air – we got some bullets in the walls of our upstairs rooms in the first two houses. We all sat together in an inside room until it was all over. We did crosswords and played cards to pass the time. That evening everything was quiet and the River empty of boats.

Letter by Margaret to her sister Joyce, Spring 1949:

Methodist Compound
39 Bah So Lu
Ningpo
Chekiang
East China

Monday, May 2

Dear Joyce,

Here I am again! And as usual with something I want doing. The balloon really has gone up now and I'm trying to write as many letters as I can before their way out is closed. We seem to have been waiting for this to happen for so long that it seems queer now it's come. I will reserve judgement about the American Baptist missionaries' views until I see for myself and at the moment I'm doubtful about them. I should think that the poor Chinese (the ordinary folk) had had enough shaking up in the last decade or so to last them a long time.

I think the trouble with the MRA (Moral Rearmament Group) in England is their American approach. But whatever you think about them you have to agree that the principles are right – they have very sound views on most subjects. Also they are trying to do something that the church until recently has almost completely neglected. It seems to me that the state of the world today is a judgement on the ordinary Christian for not trying to live up to their religion in their work. Lately I've felt very strongly that we are all to blame in this matter. I know I am. It's all very well for me to stand up in the pulpit and preach but what have I done in the staff room and classroom? I don't mean "are you saved?" etc. but just living up to Christianity. I think that's what MRA are trying to do – they may be pretty annoying, but they're on the right track and if the church members instead of just criticising tried to do the same thing we might get somewhere. We scared to try the thing out properly – I don't think this increased production do is such rot as you think – because these folk are very sincere and a lot of them are workers and I believe that if one Christian really lives out his religion big things happen. Sorry! I didn't intend to go on at such length – the situation out here's made me think pretty deeply about such matters.

Yes, we have a tennis court and play when we can – with playing with Jack and Peter I'm improving quite a bit. About time too!

About the part songs – as it happens I haven't brought many with me and I've lent them to somebody. Offhand I can't think of titles and publishers – it's such ages since I've done anything with them. The only one I remember is that humorous one – "the goslings" by Frederick Bridges (Novello in two or four parts) – it's fairly easy and very entertaining.

You're lucky to hear from Geoff – I haven't heard for ages. If you see Pat, thank her for her letter. I've put the address on the back of the letters I'm enclosing except Aunty B's which you know. Thanks a lot – with much love – Margaret

PS. I am glad you like your job so much better now – is she still going strong in your former department? Thanks very much for the photo – I think it's very good indeed. I'm awfully glad to have it.

Chapter 7: Last Days in China

Life changed overnight. No post arrived for three months. We had to report to an office in the city, taking with us a photo of ourselves, which was stuck to an alien pass. We had to carry this wherever we went. We were given a list of the things we couldn't do. One was that we were no longer free to leave Ningpo. I could still go to Kong Tong church on Sundays but no more trips into the country as before.

The people were amazed at the good behaviour of the communist troops. When Chiang Kai-shek started sending planes to bomb the city, the soldiers were very helpful aiding people whose houses were damaged. One of the buildings damaged was part of the Riverside Girls' School where Doris worked. Chiang Kai-shek originally came from Fengwa about twenty miles from Ningpo and had always been considered one of "our boys". The bombing changed all that, I remember. The first time he sent his planes over it was a Sunday, when there was a big market right in the centre of the city. We ran out when we heard the planes coming and stood in horror as about six American B24 bombers came over and dropped their bombs. There was no protection against air raids and we could hear the screams as they exploded. Ningpo became a town of the night – everything happened at night – the buses ran at night and shops stayed open all night.

I still continued to go to Kong Tong on Sunday mornings, but one day I was stopped and questioned by two army men. This made me a bit nervous, so from then on someone came with me. One Sunday planes flew over very low and we all expected bombs to fall, but nothing happened. June, July, August passed and then at the beginning of September the postman arrived with two sackfuls of letters! The communists had kept all our mail for three months. It was wonderful to read all those letters we had longed for. We had no idea if the letters we posted home were getting there. In the event we found they had been!

Jack Gedye and the three Anglican missionaries were due to leave for furlough in three weeks' time. It became clear that as a newcomer I would not be allowed to do anything. Only those who had been doing a job for so many years would be permitted to work. Doris was a schoolteacher and had been teaching for years, so she had no problems. My colleagues decided that I should leave with Jack and the others as it was obvious I wouldn't be able to do anything. They thought I should make a fresh start somewhere else. I knew they were right but was very upset at the thought of leaving China, where I had been so happy.

I began to pack up my things. I had left one trunkful and a bicycle in Hong Kong anyway, so hadn't much to take with me. Doris and I went around saying goodbye to everyone, but I still found it hard to realise I was actually going. On September 20th we went down to the bus station at night to catch a bus to Hanzhou. The Japanese had destroyed Ningpo station and railway during the war, so our only way out was to go to Hanzhou and get a train from there to Shanghai. Since the communists took over, the boats to Shanghai were no longer running either.

It was about forty miles from Ningpo to Hanzhou and the journey was fairly uneventful. We were stopped halfway and had our luggage examined – they just turned my suitcase upside down and tipped everything out! We crossed several rickety bridges over rivers en route and reached Hanzhou early in the morning. We booked on the train to go to Shanghai that evening and had a pleasant day looking at the sights of Hanzhou and doing some shopping. Then we got ourselves onto the train and I slept soundly nearly all the way to Shanghai. Jack and I were to stay at Route Culty with Gordon Ward. His wife and children had returned to

England. The first thing we had to do was to apply for permission to leave and for that we needed three Chinese people who would stand guarantor for us. Gordon took us round visiting to find people who would do this for us. I was surprised at how willingly people agreed. Then we went to the government office. They gave us our permit to leave. That done, we could go ahead and book ourselves on a boat. There was a French ship leaving Shanghai on October 10th. Those of us who were only going to Hong Kong had to travel steerage. Our Anglican friends who were going home, were able to travel in a more civilised way to Marseilles.

The day we left was a very special day in China – "the tenth day of the tenth month", the day of Sun Yat Sen's revolution in 1911. The communists decided to inaugurate the People's Republic of China on that day. There was a three-mile procession in Shanghai which no one was allowed to cross; we just managed to beat it in our taxi to the quay. When we got on board, we found there was a communist Band on the quay, playing us off. One of the tunes they played was "The British Grenadiers": they probably thought it was a communist song. As the boat pulled away I wept. Would I ever see China again? I felt so sad about leaving.

Travelling steerage was quite an adventure. We slept in bunks in troop accommodation and mixed with all sorts of people. We were in the women's hold: nuns, missionaries, Eurasians, prostitutes et cetera. There were no plugs in the wash basins and the lavatories were completely public – a mighty rushing stream ran through the room held in by a wooden barrier which you balanced on and hoped you wouldn't fall in. Fortunately, Molly Churchill and the Duddingtons let us use their toilets. We stood up to eat and sat on the floor on deck as there were no chairs. It was good that we only had two days and two nights on that ship. On October 12th we landed in Hong Kong just five days before all air, train and shipping services between communist China and Hong Kong were suspended. My China adventure was over – what next?

Chapter 8: The Road to India

In Hong Kong we found a lot of mail piled up for us - letters from the Mission House showed they still hadn't understood the situation. One letter read "we don't understand why Margaret is leaving when she's doing so well at Chinese." My reaction was the very next morning to send a cable saying, "BUDD WILLING ANYWHERE".

I was in Hong Kong for about four weeks. It was at least two weeks before I got a response from the Mission House to my cable and letter. I received a cable in reply telling me to "proceed Bengal". I was pleased at that because my younger brother was working in Calcutta. He left Kingswood School in 1944 and went into the army and trained with the Officers Corps. He was in the Royal Engineers and was sent to India to build Bailey bridges. He was demobbed in 1948 and went home, but before he left India he landed a job with a British firm in Calcutta and was engaged for a while to a girl called Pat – he had lost all desire to go to university, much to my parents' disappointment. I hadn't seen him for five years and now I was going to meet him again.

Jack Gedye was sailing on the P&O Liner, Carthage, and I got a berth to Bombay on the same boat. It was due to sail at the end of October. We made the most of our time in Hong Kong, seeing the sights, visiting friends and shopping. We hadn't been sent the whole of our salary in China because of the inflation so we received it now and I was able to buy a typewriter.

Hong Kong was bursting at the seams with Chinese refugees, missionaries who were waiting to see what happened, and all sorts of other people. The Sailors and Soldiers home was turned into a hotel for missionaries of all varieties and nationalities. The kitchen was kept busy feeding us all. Most Missionary Societies and Boards couldn't bring themselves to believe that China was closing to missionaries. While we were in Hong Kong the China Inland Mission tried to fly about twenty missionaries into China, but they were not allowed to land. In the event most of us had to choose somewhere else to work. Many decided to go home, but most of us were to be found working all over the world in the next few years.

The voyage to Bombay took about ten days and was very different from our experience on the Lancashire. There were stewardesses who looked after our needs and everything was organised. There was a swimming pool and a creche for the small children. Passengers didn't get asked to do anything! We docked at Bombay on November 10th. I said goodbye to Jack Gedye. Later he became a Minister in the Midlands. He had been born in China and had married his wife there. He died in 1969. I never saw him again.

I was met from the ship by the Reverend Noel Brewis who was returning to India after leave and was staying with the Reverend and Mrs Thorne, who were our representatives in Bombay. I only had one night in Bombay, so didn't see much of the city. Noel put me on the train to Calcutta before he went to catch his to Secunderabad in South India. He was so knowledgeable about trains that the very nice lady I was sharing a coupé with thought he must be working for the railway!

On the morning of November 13th the train ran into Howrah station at Calcutta and there waiting for me was my brother, Geoffrey. It was marvellous to see him again after five years.

He collected me and all my luggage and took me to 16 Sudder Street where I was staying with the Reverend and Mrs Arfon Roberts. He promised to come and take me out for a meal that evening and then went off to his office in the city. I found that Mr Roberts was going up to Bankura for pre-Synod committee meetings the next day and he wanted to talk to me about my position. The Mission House had written to him saying that I would only be in Bengal temporarily because they were sure that in about six months the dust would have settled in China and I would be going back! So I wasn't to learn Bengali, but they were to find me a job in English. I told Arfon in no uncertain terms that they were wrong, that I certainly wouldn't get back to China and that I expected to learn Bengali and get stuck into being a missionary in Bengal. I was pleased when I saw that he believed me rather than the Mission House. He said this would make a difference to what he would say about me at the Women's Work Committee in Bankura. When he returned, he told me the committee took me at my word and that I was to go to Sarenga and start learning Bengali. Jessica English and Lorna Wood arrived at Sudder Street to do their Christmas shopping and I travelled back with them a few days later. Chandrakona Road was the station nearest to Sarenga – it was a hundred and ten miles from Calcutta. We travelled on a passenger train which stopped at every station – about twenty-five of them – and took seven hours to get there. Then we caught a bus to take us twenty-one miles to Sarenga. The road in those days was terrible, just a dirt road full of potholes and ruts. It took us over three hours to get to Sarenga. I was taken to the nurses' bungalow where I was to live for the time being and was able at last to unpack properly.

The first few months in India were very hard for me. I was homesick for China and the Bengal Christians were very different from the Chinese. The enthusiasm and initiative of the Chinese Christians seemed to me completely lacking. I kept getting letters from the Mission House telling me I would soon be back in China and insisting that I keep up my Chinese language study. This didn't make things very easy for me and I was quite miserable and unsettled.

Jessica English realised what I was going through. She was in charge of the Girls' hostel, but in the school holidays she was doing some pastoral work in the Santal Mission Circuit across the river from Sarenga. There most of the Christians belonged to a tribal group called the Santals. The schools had broken up for the Puja holidays. There were always holidays in the autumn because it was time for many Hindu festivals. Puja means worship or religious festival and all the schools and government offices were on holiday. Within a few days Jessica was going on a three-week pastoral visit to the Santal Mission Circuit and she invited me to join her. I jumped at the chance and had a marvellous time with her: visiting the people and joining in meetings and services. Of course I couldn't talk to anybody, but Jessica was always on hand to help me. I got to know and love the Santal people – they were much more like the Chinese in their attitudes than most Bengalis and I knew this was where I would like to work.

I had to battle with the Mission House about learning Bengali. They didn't want to give me a grant to attend the language school at Darjeeling, presumably still believing that I would be returning to China. I wrote an impassioned letter to Miss Alice Walton, who was the secretary for Women's Work at the Methodist Missionary Society. I told her everything and explained why I knew I couldn't return to China. She stuck up for me and I got my grant. In April I travelled to Darjeeling by train for the three-month language school that was held there every year. Travelling with me was Phyllis Hunt, the new missionary nurse, who had arrived in Sarenga in February. We all worked very hard at the language, reading the set books and practising talking with the Bengali teachers. I was very intrigued by the many different accents amongst the students – American and European, Australian, not to mention Yorkshire, Scottish etc., in which Bengali was spoken! No wonder the Bengalis had trouble understanding us!

My post was being sent on to me and I was delighted to receive several letters from China. Doris wrote to me and told me what was happening. The communists were keen on "soul-searching" days. They ran one at Doris's school. All the staff had to confess their sins and reveal their wrong thoughts about things. Lily Wu wrote me a lovely letter in which she said this: "I hope you won't feel that all that effort you put into learning Chinese is wasted. I don't think God wastes anything". I never got a chance to use Chinese again and I was now working hard at Bengali.

We had a quiet day at the language school. At one session we were asked to share how God had called us to India. When it came to my turn I said that I had never thought of India, that I had always felt called to China and now, thanks to the communists, I had finished up in Bengal and had mixed feelings about it. Someone responded: "Ah vocation by push!" How true.

Halfway through our three months at the language school we had a week off for half term. There was to be an opportunity to trek into the Himalayan foothills and to a height of 12,000 feet, staying each night at dak Bungalows, which had belonged to the British Mail Service. Greatly daring, I put my name down to go and about fifteen of us made up the party. We employed Nepali coolies to carry our bedding and the food we would need. It was a wonderful experience. We covered between twelve and seventeen miles each day and the path was very up and down, often descending two to three thousand feet and climbing up again on the other side. We visited Buddhist temples with their prayer flags and wheels and passed through many villages. We saw plenty of livestock, including yaks. About the third day we reached Sandakphu, 12,000 feet up – our highest point. The coolies always reached the bungalows first because they didn't use the contour path but went straight up the bank. So by the time we arrived they had fires burning and water boiling. We were told that if we got up at dawn the next morning we would see the sunrise over the Himalayas. Someone set an alarm and at 3 a.m. we wrapped up well and went outside into the freezing cold. As we waited with chattering teeth we wondered if it was worth it – and then, suddenly just as though a switch had been thrown, the whole panorama of the Himalayas lit up with a pink glow. It took your breath away; it was so wonderful. Gradually the light faded and we could only see Kanchenjunga. We were glad to get inside and warm up with breakfast. That day we had an eleven-mile walk to Phellut. All the way along the path were rhododendrons in their natural habitat, all the colours of the rainbow. That night it poured with rain and we awoke to a thick mist, so no sunrise view that morning and a very wet walk back to Sandakphu. No view there either, so we were very lucky to see it when we did. After this we gradually worked our way to lower levels and reached Darjeeling after a week's walking - about a hundred and twenty miles altogether.

Whilst we were in Darjeeling an invitation came from the Roman Catholic seminary in Kurseong, halfway down the hill, to join them for a fellowship day and discussion on Church unity. It was the time of Pope John XXIII and Vatican II, when the Catholic Church addressed its relation to the modern world. A party of us went and we had a great day together comparing Catholic and Protestant thought on all sorts of subjects. This of course, was something new to us and we were thrilled at the warmth of the friendship we received.

There had been a very dry few months until the beginning of June when the monsoon broke. We then had thirty-seven inches of rain in three days – more than a whole year's rainfall in the British Isles. As a result, there were landslips all over the place. Down the hill from the Language School was the Mount Herman estate where many missionary families stayed. Many of the missionary wives who had children at Mount Herman school stayed on in term time. Several of their bungalows were flattened by the slips. We learned later that Darjeeling was cut off from below by a huge landslide which had destroyed a whole section of the railway and the road, so it was going to be some time before we could think of leaving. It was the beginning of July when we were able to leave. We took a taxi to the big landslide where steps had been cut into the hillside and a rope banister constructed. We had to climb up one side of the landslide and then down. Then another taxi took us to Kurseong where we could get the little train down to Siliguri on the plains. Here we caught the train to Calcutta. Because of partition between

India and Pakistan, the railway which used to be the main route to Darjeeling and Assam was now in East Pakistan and could not be used. The Indians had built a new railway called the Assam link. It involved crossing the Ganges by boat and travelling along newly constructed embankments. On these, which were decidedly unsteady, the train couldn't go more than fifteen miles an hour. At last we were back in Calcutta and I was soon on the way back to Sarenga.

In August I went to Calcutta and sat my first Bengali exam, which I passed. I then spent three months in Bankura living with Miss Josephine Sewell. The "powers that be" thought Bankura would be a better place to prepare for my second and last Bengali exam. I visited families in the Christian village there and gave some addresses to the women's meeting. In China I had preached in Chinese two or three times and taken assembly in the school next door, so it was a bit hard to go through it all again. But Bengali was much easier to learn than Chinese and I progressed quite quickly. It is a Sanskrit language and therefore quite like Latin, which I had learned at school. I never thought that Latin would be so useful. I was always hopeless at French at school, but I now discovered that I was good at languages. I returned to Sarenga in February and in May I went on my first hill holiday to Ootacamund in the Nilgiri hills in South India. My two closest friends Stella Bailey and Win Taylor were missionaries in Mysore and I used to join them at Mysore Cottage in Ootacamund. Most of my hot weather holidays during my twenty years in India were spent there. On my way back I stopped in Calcutta to take my second Bengali exam and passed easily. One of my tests was to preach a ten-minute sermon on a given text with just twenty minutes to prepare. Having passed, I was out of probation and could start my missionary career. I packed up and moved over the river to Deuli in the Santal Mission Circuit. It was June 1951 and I had a room in the Deuli bungalow sharing the home of the Reverend and Mrs Burton, Wilf and Gwen. Wilf had arranged for a young woman called Soilabala Hansda to be my companion. She became my closest friend. She had been married, but her young husband had died of tuberculosis after only a year of marriage. She decided she didn't want to remarry because she felt God was calling her to serve in the church.

Visiting the villages

Chapter 9: The Santal Mission

From 1951 until 1957, with a break for furlough in 1953, I was a pastoral worker in the Santal Mission Circuit. The circuit covered an area of about eight hundred and fifty square miles and went right up to the borders of Bihar state. There was a mixture of tribal and Bengali villages with a good number of Christians amongst the villagers. There were three main Christian centres – Samadi, Polasboni and Bagdubi, and Barikul. At each of these centres mud-built rest houses had been built for visitors to stay in, but the one at Polasboni had been burned down by an extreme Hindu group, known as the Hindu Seva Sangha. After I came to the circuit this group were not much in evidence. Deuli, where the Mission bungalow was, lay about eight miles from Sarenga but further still from the Santal area of the circuit. It had been an indigo plantation. The mission bought it together with the plantation house. The circuit had been established as a result of outreach work from Sarenga and, as more and more converts were made, it separated from Sarenga to become a circuit on its own.

Our first outing was to the Quarterly Meeting which was being held at Barikul. The villages took it in turns to supply the food and it was Deuli's turn. It was a rather hot and sultry day and we had got about halfway when clouds began to form. Soila said, "I think there's going to be a storm. We had better hurry or we won't be able to cross the Bashi Kal." I was amazed as the Bashi Kal was a stream which usually had very little water in it or none at all. I had not been in the Santal Mission during the rains, so had never seen it in full flood. It soon began to rain quite heavily and we took refuge in a Santal village called Sarasdanga. The villagers brought us tea and sat and talked to us. After an hour or so the storm ended and we went to look at the Kal which was near the village. To my amazement it was now a mighty rushing stream. The bullock cart couldn't cross and nor could we. I learned that day that in a storm at least an inch or two of rain would fall. Kali, the bullock cart driver, was all for going back to Deuli, but Soila said, "no, we can stay the night here." I said, "but we don't know each other and it's not a Christian village." Soila responded, "that doesn't matter. They will be glad to put us up. By early tomorrow morning we can go across." I learned to trust Soila's judgement. She was quite right – Sarasdanga was delighted to offer us hospitality. They opened up their little schoolhouse and brought us mats and string beds to sleep on. They insisted on cooking for us and let us use our own food. We had a lovely meal; they killed two chickens for us. Then they lit a fire and we all sat around it and talked. They asked us to sing to them and Soila and I preached. This was my first experience of village hospitality and it wasn't the last time I took advantage of it in the years that lay ahead. The next morning, we were up at dawn and were soon in Barikul. The hungry delegates had guessed what had happened and were glad to know that lunch was secure!

This was 1951 and I wasn't due for furlough until December 1952. So I was able to establish myself in the Santal mission before leaving. I spent my time travelling around the circuit visiting the Christian families and preaching in Bengali every Sunday. I also established women's meeting at all the churches. As there was no one who spoke English I had to do everything in Bengali. This was marvellous and I was soon quite eloquent. I realised I was going to have to learn Santali, the tribal language, and resolved to start that when I returned from leave. My friendship with Soila deepened. She was a lovely person, aged about twenty-one when she came to be my companion. Through her I learned so much about the people and their customs and culture. She was completely honest and open with me and would answer my questions about anything.

The Reverend Wilfred Burton was my superintendent during

the first two years and his second-in-command was the Reverend Santosh Kisku, who lived in Samadi about ten miles further on from Barikul. The Burtons had their first child, Rosemary, in 1951. Wilfred and Gwen learned Santali and didn't know Bengali. This didn't matter in the Santal Mission as the people were all bilingual. One of the things that surprised me was the way in which the children could use two or three languages with ease, in contrast to the way people in Britain find foreign languages so difficult. Missionaries' children too were adept at picking up Bengali and using English as well.

I soon realised that there had been very little teaching of the faith, particularly among the women and I thanked God that my experience in China was a pattern for what I wanted to do in Bengal. I started giving Soila Bible teaching so that she too could help in this work. She told me she had always wanted to be a Biblewoman and I was able to guide her into making an application to the Synod to have training for the role. The Synod were excited about this and advertised in the various circuits for any other women who were interested. Before I left for home two other women applied – Mrs Promila Kisku whose husband had been a catechist in Sarenga before he died of tuberculosis, and Miss Romoni Gorai, a young girl of eighteen who had read to class 6 in school. It was arranged that when I returned they were to live near me and I would train them.

My brother, Geoffrey, had been home on leave. He had become engaged again. The plan was for the knot to be tied at Sudder Street Methodist Church. His wife to be was Joyce Thompson, originally from Rotherham, who worked as a comptometer operator at Alcan Industries Ltd. in Banbury. My parents had befriended her when she moved down from Yorkshire, and she often came to their home. Geoffrey met her there. She came to India in September 1952 and stayed with Harry and Joy Smith at 14/2 Sudder Street. Joy stood in as the bride's mother and I was to be the bridesmaid. I had missed my sister's wedding in 1951 so it was good to be at my brother's.

The Minister who married them was one of our missionaries, the Reverend Lloyd Pocklington – Pock to his friends, who was the minister at Sudder Street that year. I came to Calcutta for this event straight from being out in the villages and felt a bit like a fish out of water.

At my brother's wedding Sudder Street Methodist Church 1952

At this point I sailed for England on furlough and was home for about a year. My parents were now living in Banbury where my father was Superintendent. I travelled up and down the country speaking at Missionary meetings. I mostly spoke about my experience in China. I was exasperated that so many people thought the church was finished in China just because there were no longer missionaries there. I was at pains to tell them that the Chinese Church didn't depend on missionaries and that it would survive and grow. I didn't believe that the movement of the spirit I had experienced in Ningpo could die. I was a bit cross with the Mission

House because they seemed to have lost interest in China. It was only much later that I learned how the returned missionaries from China had criticised the Home Boards. I had missed all that with not coming home at the time, but I had no regrets as I was now wedded to the Bengal District and had a job waiting there.

In November 1953 I returned to India by sea. To fly never occurred to us then; that came much later. I was not a good sailor but had learned to control it. My brother was no longer in India. He and Joyce had returned home, and he eventually got a job with Alcan Industries, where he worked for the rest of his life.

I was soon back in Deuli and had a new superintendent, the Reverend John Hastings. He and his wife, Joyce, had their first child, Christine. She was about the same age as my sister's little girl Helen and so became my adopted niece. One of the nice things about the missionaries in the Bengal district was our close family relationship. We single missionaries never felt left out and we were Bengal aunties to all the children, who to this day treat us as one of the family.

The Quarterly Meeting had suggested I should leave Deuli and live more in the centre of the circuit. It was decided I should move to Barikul, which I did early in 1954. Promila, Soila and Romoni also came to live there in what used to be the pastor's house. We divided our time between the Biblewomen's training and travelling around the circuit. We would spend about ten days in the rest house at Samadi visiting all the villages around there taking services and meetings and, if we were asked, visiting non-Christian villages to preach. I had been taught that it was wrong to start "arguments" when you were preaching. You had to present the gospel and the congregation would either take it or leave it. But I soon discovered that the Indian mind worked differently. They liked a discussion and the Bengali word for discussion was frequently translated as argument. Often people said, "If you can take us to the last boundary of discussion, we will believe." One day I was going to Bankura for a committee meeting. I had to leave Barikul at 3 a.m.

and walk six miles to a village called Phulkusma where I would catch a bus at 6 a.m. When I reached Phulkusma I bought myself a cup of tea and sat in the Ladies' seat on the bus. Suddenly the door opened and a man got in and sat by me. "I've come to have a religious discussion with you," he said. He turned out to be a member of the Jain sect, who are vegetarian and believe that God is in everything. He started by asking me if I believed that God is in everything. I replied that I did, but I didn't think I meant the same as he did. He said, "I am God. You are God. A goat is God, so how can you eat it?" So the discussion continued. Then I told him that there was a very cold land in the North were people lived. Nothing would grow, so there were no vegetables or crops. So what could the people eat but fish or whale-meat? At that moment two men who had sat in the front seat started clapping and saying, "She's won! She's won! The Miss sahib has won." I was taken aback and so was the Jain, who got off the bus and disappeared. I felt terribly guilty, but three months later when I went to catch the bus again, the Jain was there with some companions from his village. He invited me to visit his village for a proper discussion and please could I give them some copies of the Christian Scriptures! This incident taught me a lesson which I never forgot.

Soila, Romoni and Promila and I had our adventures. On one occasion we went to catch a bus from Jhilimili, a place about three miles from Samadi, at about 7 a.m. When we got to Jhilimili we found there was going to be no bus that day. It was the first Sunday in the New Year and I was due to take the Covenant Service at a village called Jalneja. We were told that the bus had gone on a picnic! It was twenty-two miles to Jalneja and we decided to walk. The two men who were carrying our luggage were game, so off we went. We got to Jalneja at about three in the afternoon. They had kept food for us, which was just as well as we were very hungry. After the meal we had the Covenant Service and visited all the Christian homes in the village. We stayed the night and went on to another village the next day.

I became very concerned about the position of women in the church. I had started women's meetings in the different villages. The meetings in turn had appointed secretaries. I suggested that the Women's Fellowship secretaries should become members of the Leaders' Meetings and this was agreed. Some of the women asked if we could have a Women's Convention for all the women in the circuit and I agreed to organise one. In 1955 we held the first one in Barikul. It was well advertised and we thought perhaps fifty women would come. In the event over ninety came and we had to send out for more rice! Jessica English was the main speaker that year and between sessions there was singing and dancing Santal fashion. There was unanimous demand that we should have a convention every year and I promised to arrange the next one.

I was busy learning Santali and had been to Dumka to take my first exam. Dumka was the centre of the Lutheran Santal Mission. It was in Bihar province in the area known as the Santal Parganas. This was a tribal protected area with land reserved for the Santals. In 1857, the year of the Indian mutiny, the Santals had their own rebellion – not against the British but against their rapacious Bengali landlords. The Bengali landlords were getting Santals into debt in order to get possession of their land and push them into serfdom. The British hastily quashed the rebellion because they needed all their force against the Indian Mutiny, which Indians call the first war of Indian Independence. The British then established a protectorate over all the tribal areas, covering Assam, Bihar, Bengal and Orissa. The Lutherans, from Scandinavia and the USA, were the first missionaries to work amongst the Santals. They worked out a Romanised alphabet for the language and started publishing books in Santali, including the Bible. It was these books which I had to study for my exam – there was one about the history of the Santals, another about their customs and culture, and a third comprised the memoirs of a village head, which he had dictated himself. It was all very interesting, but nobody really knows about the origins of the tribe. Their language belongs to the oldest language group in the world and has a fiendishly difficult grammar and construction! Very different from either Chinese or Bengali. I passed my first exam and bought the books to prepare for the second.

One result of my learning Santali was that Synod appointed me as a delegate to the Santal Christian Council. The other delegate was my colleague, John Hastings, who was learning Hindi and Santali as well as Bengali. This meant that I got to know all the other churches and their leaders, national and missionary. One of the people I met was a Norwegian lady called Hilda Mildur. She was in her sixties and had worked for years with Santal women. I invited her to be the speaker at our next Women's Convention in 1956 and was delighted when she accepted.

In January 1956 we arranged for the Convention to be held at Bagdubi where they had recently built a new church. We built temporary houses of straw and bamboo to shelter all the women – over a hundred came to this one. Miss Mildur was a triumph. She used flannelgraph for her presentation, not to tell stories as flannelgraph was normally used, but to demonstrate Christian symbols. She got the women participating in a marvellous way and there were several conversions. We unanimously invited her to come to Samadi in 1957.

Meanwhile news was reaching other circuits about our successful conventions. "Can we come and join in?" Was the cry from Sarenga, Bankura, Calcutta and Barrackpore. I had to say "No," as I knew we couldn't cope with any more people. But I promised to help them run their own conventions. I started with Sarenga and we ran a very successful one in 1956 with myself as the speaker. This was followed by one in Bankura with Miss Stella Beare of the United Church of North India as the speaker. In 1957 as well as our own Santal mission convention at Samadi we ran another in Calcutta and yet another in Barrackpore. The whole thing snowballed and at the Synod, before I went on leave at the end of 1957 it was decided that we needed a district organisation for women, and that I should be the District Organiser, to start work

71

when I returned from furlough. So ended my appointment solely in the Santal mission, I didn't lose contact with them of course, but I now had to spread myself over the whole district. The new organisation was to be called the Mohila Samiti which means Women's Fellowship. Promila, Soila and Romoni were now fully trained women workers. Promila went to work in Sarenga and Soila and Romoni were to carry on the work in the Santal mission.

Sarenga, 1958

Chapter 10: One More Step

My leave in 1958 turned out to be a sad one. My brother's little daughter died of cancer. She was only four and a half years old. Their second child, a boy, was just born when the cancer was discovered. Margaret Jane's funeral took place on December 9th, 1958. I sailed for India ten days later.

This time I was to live with Enid Blears at a place called Raniganj. This was in an industrial area near the city of Asansole. It was also on the Bengal coalfield. It was not so central to the rest of the Bengal District and so meant more travelling for me. I was now faced with a new job which I had to work out for myself. I decided to visit all the Circuits and meet the women and find out all I could about them. So here I will list the various Circuits, all of which I got to know very well in the next four years.

The Santal Mission Circuit was my first love, where most of the Christians were tribal Santals. Sarenga was the Circuit next door, six miles across the River Kasai. It had been evangelised from Bankura forty miles away. The Methodist Church was well established in Sarenga – there were schools, a teacher training college, Boys' and Girls' Hostels, a hospital and a rather beautiful Indian-style Church building. I had already held two women's conventions in Sarenga; there were plenty of women there able to take a leadership role. Bankura was also well developed. The main institution was Bankura Christian College which had university status. There was a high school for boys and one for girls, and a boys' and girls' hostel. There was also a hostel for women university students. The Chairman lived in Bankura and the District Office was there. There was a Christian village on the outskirts of the town.

73

Bankura town itself was the political centre of the District of Bankura so there were law-courts etc. and the residence of the District Commissioner. There was also a Leprosy Mission Home.

Calcutta was where the Methodist Work began in the 19th century. A Missionary who was an Army Chaplain set about building Sudder Street Methodist Church about a hundred and fifty years before. Some of the Sudder Street Church members started work among the Bengali population and towards the end of the 19th Century Taltolla Methodist Church was built right in the centre of the city. Soon other churches were founded on the outskirts of Calcutta. Missionaries were sent out to help in the work. An offshoot of Calcutta was begun a few miles up the Eastern Railway at Barrackpore. The Anglicans had a chaplaincy for the troops who were stationed there. They had built a church and later a Bishop was consecrated. Methodist work concentrated on the Bengali population who lived in Barrackpore and also a mission was started to work among Hindi-speaking factory workers in the paper factory at Tittaghur and later at other factories founded in the area. A bungalow was bought on the banks of the River Hoogli for a missionary family to live in. Next door was a house for the Bengali Minister and his family. Just on the opposite bank of the Hoogli was Serampore College founded by the famous Baptist missionary William Carey.

The railway was constructed from Calcutta via Bankura into Uttar Pradesh in about 1860. Missionaries went from Calcutta to Bankura to serve among the navvies and thus the Bengali work in Bankura began. Later in the century activity spread to Sarenga and over the river to the Santal Mission.

Another circuit began at Madhupur much further up the railway. This was a centre for railways in the east of India. By the time the railways were established, there was a large population of Anglo-Indians. Mission activity began here through Anglo-Indian families who moved up from Calcutta, but Bengali work also flourished. From here work began at Kano, another tribal area where Santals lived. Raniganj began with Chaplaincy work amongst English workers and the Leprosy Mission founded a Leprosy Home there in 1893.

While I was living in Raniganj the British began to build a steel plant in a new town called Durgapur. Several hundred villages were cleared from jungle over a wide area and in no time a city grew up. Apart from the Steel Plant various other factories were established and a forest of bungalows were being built. Initially the population was comprised mostly of foreigners, who came to build the factories, but soon people from all over India came to get jobs. Eventually a Church was built – it was called a United Church but the Methodists ran it. In the same building the Mar-Thoma Church members held their services and their Minister worked with us.

I served in all these circuits: Santal Mission, Sarenga, Bankura, Calcutta, Barrackpore, Madhupur, Raniganj and Durgapur. They were all very different and it was very interesting getting to know them all. When Jessica English retired I moved into her quarters in the Women's Work bungalow in Bankura, which was much more central for me.

In my first year we organised a Convention in all the Circuits, got to know all the women, found out who would make good leaders and appointed secretaries for the different groups. I asked them to organise women's meetings in the different churches. I found them all as keen as mustard to get going. There's no doubt I had come along at the right psychological moment for the women. We fixed a date for a District Women's Fellowship Committee which the secretaries would attend. I asked them all to bring one other woman with them so that there would be two from each Circuit. We arranged to meet in Bankura in the middle of November. The whole Committee turned out, and we went for two days. My father and mother were in the Banbury Circuit at the time and my mother persuaded the Sisterhood at Marlborough Road Methodist Church in Banbury to raise some money to support my efforts. It meant that I had enough in hand to pay travel expenses to the delegates and to feed them while they were in Bankura. The meeting was a great success. The women themselves suggested that we should send two representatives to the District Synod and also that the Women's Fellowship meeting secretaries should be members of the local church leaders' meetings. We agreed to hold this Central Committee every year in November and that each circuit should write a report on their work to be sent to me as District Secretary. I would see that a resumé of these would be included in the Annual District Report. We were off! This was November, 1960.

During the years that followed we received a lot of help from women's leaders of other denominations. One of these was an Anglican lady called Ann Biswas, who came and spoke at a number of our Conventions. She wrote a number of hymns and her singing and teaching of new songs was very popular. I also got invited to speak at get-togethers for other churches and this gave us a wider outlook. All this time, negotiations towards a United Church in North India were going on, but didn't come to fruition until 1971 when I had left India. But we certainly helped prepare for it.

In January 1963, I at last managed to organise a training Conference for all the women leaders in the District. It was held at Samadi in the Santal Mission Circuit and the tribal women were delighted to host it. Everyone foregathered at Bankura and we hired a bus to take is to Samadi – it held fifty-three of us. At the request of Nandalal Murmu, the head of the village school, who was in charge of catering, we took with us an unfortunate goat, who provided the meat for our meals. The Samadi women had prepared leafy bowers surrounding holes in the ground as toilets, and also bamboo shelters behind which the townswomen could bathe. In the event the latter were hardly used as everyone wanted to join the village women to bathe in the village "tank". Every village had a "tank" which was really like a lake formed by building an earth bund which captured the water from local streams and the rain, and was used for everything – washing clothes, bathing, washing cattle. I was amazed at how much the people from Calcutta, Barrackpore and Madhupur enjoyed being in the country. Some of them had never been in a village before. Ann Biswas joined us as the main speaker. Stella Bailey, from Mysore, was staying with me and she came along and joined in. She taught them how to cut out and make stuffed animals. During a session when we sang hymns in different languages, she taught us one in Kanarese. We had sessions on how to run meetings, keep minutes, find speakers, even how to give talks on the Bible. I think we were all sorry when, after three days, the bus arrived to take us home. Some of the Santal women cried when they said goodbye.

Because I had learned Santali I was made a delegate to the Santal Christian Council and attended their annual assembly. I was elected secretary to their Christian Home Committee and we published a number of booklets about families and the home. They organised Christian Home Conferences which were attended by men and women of the various churches working among the Santals. I remember the first one which was held in Benagaria, a Lutheran centre. We had a session about arranged marriages. Because so many young people were working in places like Durgapur, Calcutta and Asansole things were going wrong. Village mothers and fathers were arranging marriages in the old manner, using village people as go-betweens. They didn't go to see what was going on with their young people. As a result, disasters were happening – a new bride would go to join her husband and find he already had a woman in residence! Parents were tending to arrange for marriages only when their sons were older because they relied on the financial help they gave for the education of the younger children. The boys were lonely and ready for marriage and so formed their own relationships. I had warned parents that this might happen, but usually they didn't want to believe it. "My boy would never do that!"

So I did this session to try to get them to think about it. I asked them which they approved of – love matches or arranged marriages. "Arranged marriages, of course, because love matches always go wrong." I asked them how marriages were going in their villages and they admitted that quite a few came to grief. "Were they arranged marriages?" I asked – "Yes," they said. They realised they weren't thinking straight and we eventually had a good discussion on how times were changing and what could be done about it. One of our Christian families in a village called Kasmar had a son, Babanandam, who was a chief inspector in the Delhi police. They arranged a match for Babanandam without telling him and then wrote and told him to come home to get married. He replied, saying that he could not marry an uneducated village girl as he needed a wife to help him in his career, who could entertain visitors and so on. The father was furious with him and said that the girl didn't need to go to Delhi, she could live with them and be a help to his wife. Babanandam could come on leave and start babies! It was a clash of cultures. Actually Babanandam had already chosen a wife, a Christian girl, a trained teacher from Sarenga. In the end the father was forced to give in and Babanandam and Romola were married in Sarenga. It's been a very successful marriage.

I was also secretary of the Bengal Christian Council Christian Home Committee and was able to go to the National Christian Council Christian Home Committee in Nagpur. So my knowledge of what was happening in the wider church in India increased greatly. From Nagpur I was sent to an All-India Christian Home Conference held at the YWCA House in Ootacamund in 1961. That was a great experience for me, meeting people from all over India. That same year I went to a North East India Christian Home Conference held in Shillong, the capital of Assam province, about Family Planning. It was very interesting to meet delegations from the various tribal groups, Nagas, Khasis and many others. The Assam tribals are mostly Christian and were mainly evangelised by Welsh Presbyterian missionaries. The Khasis sing like the Welsh too.

As the time drew near for my next furlough I began to wonder about my next step. I felt the Women's Fellowship work was going well and wasn't going to need me much longer. Then out of the

Santal Women's Convention, Barikul, 1955

blue came an invitation from the Northern Evangelical Lutheran Church to teach at the Santal Theological Seminary in Benegaria. They were affiliating to Serampore College and needed another member of staff with a degree, to be able to enter students for the Licentiate of Theology under Serampore. After much thought and prayer, the request came to the Bengal District Synod and they agree to lend me to the Lutherans. So when I went on leave in March 1963 I knew I would be moving from Bengal into Bihar.

Chapter 11: Pastures New

While in England in 1963 I candidated for the Wesley Deaconess Order. I was accepted and spent six weeks of the autumn term at the college in Ilkley. I was glad I was able to do this as I got to know the students and also quite a few deaconesses who came to stay while I was there. It was good to be able to do some study and I had a go at learning Greek. I became very friendly with Sister Anne Bradfield, a friendship which has lasted.

During my time in Ilkley, along with three other deaconesses, I joined a party going to Germany for what was known as the European Methodist Convocation. This was held at Freudenstadt in the Black Forest on the subject of the "Christian in Society". Sister Eileen Gaunt and I were sent by the Missionary Society and Sister Marjorie Lewis and Sister Lois Tate by the Deaconess Order. This meeting was a great experience for me and was my first introduction to Methodism in Europe. Dr Lesley Davison and the Reverend Kenneth Greet were there from the Home Mission Division and the Division of Social Responsibility as well as Methodists from both sides of the Iron Curtain. We were enchanted with the beauty of the Black Forest and its wildlife. European Methodists were anxious to learn from us how we worked in society: for many of them it was something new.

I returned home to my parents in Bournemouth at the beginning of December. I was sailing for India in January and it was arranged that my Ordination Service as a deaconess take place in Calcutta in February. I already had my ordination Bible, duly inscribed, packed to take with me. The Church in Bengal had specially asked for me to be ordained in India and not in the UK. I sailed from Liverpool on January 14th on an Anchor Line boat. There were several Indian families on board and about a dozen missionaries. We celebrated Indian Republic Day on January 26th. Some of us joined with the Indians to give a concert and sang "Jona Gona Mona", the Indian national anthem, together. After one night in Bombay I embarked on the Calcutta Mail train, spending two nights on board, and then arrived at Howrah station in Calcutta. My first job in Calcutta was to buy a white sari and have a navy blouse made for my ordination on February 2nd at Tatalla Church. The old Methodist service book had been translated into Bengali by the Reverend AM Spencer who had been a missionary in Bengal for many years and had been Chairman of the District. He had translated the whole lot, including the Deaconess Ordination Service. This was used for the first and last time at my ordination! I was quite overcome by the gifts I received. Mrs Magda Krogh, the wife of the Danish principal of the College at Benagaria, who had come to Calcutta to meet me and to attend the service, gave me a leather-bound Santali New Testament. Apart from that I had some beautiful brassware dishes and some theology books and an Indian Church History. It was a very moving service led by the Reverend C.C. Pande, our beloved Bengali chairman. The choir from Sudder Street Methodist Church sang an anthem for me. It seemed that half the District had come to Calcutta for the occasion. Now I was truly a Deaconess!

Two days later Magda and I went to Sealdah station and caught a passenger train to Rampur Hat, the nearest station to Benagaria. My new life was to begin. I knew very little about the Lutheran mission which served the Northern Evangelical Lutheran Church. Their missionaries were from Norway, Denmark, Sweden and Americans, of Scandinavian origin, from the USA. I soon learned that they largely lived in the past and that they never agreed with each other. The Danes were the most up-to-date. Johannes Thoft Krogh, my principal and his wife Magda were true scholars who wanted to bring the Lutheran ministers into the twentieth century, and it was their idea to link this country seminary with Serampore

College. When William Carey founded Serampore College at the beginning of the nineteenth century he had a vision of it being a university which could give degrees. Now, of course, other universities have come into being but they didn't offer Theology. All the theological seminaries in India worth their salt are now affiliated to Serampore College which were able to give university degrees in theological subjects. At the Santal Theological Seminary where I was going to teach they were studying for the Serampore LTh (Licentiate of Theology), now upgraded to BTh and taught in the vernacular. The BD is taught in English.

I had arrived towards the end of the college year and didn't actually start teaching until July when the new college year began, so I had plenty of time for preparation. Johs, Magda and I discussed the programme for the coming year. I was to teach early Church History, Indian Church History, English and the Life and Letters of St Paul. So began an interesting four years. The students were mainly from the Lutheran Church and, as Santals, mostly had a village background. We also had students from the Baptist Church in Dinajpur, Bengal and Assam. We had one woman student for the Licenciate of Theology, Elbina Murmu, the wife of the General Superintendent of the Northern Evangelical Lutheran Church. Apart from the LTh students we had a few who had not taken, or passed, the School Leaving Examination, and would take our own exam at the end of the course. We also ran a course for the students' wives and there were two women members of staff who looked after that.

We began with morning prayers in the chapel each day at 7 a.m., then:

7.30 – 8.30   classes
8.30 – 9.30   classes
9.30 – 10.30   classes

After this I'd go home for breakfast, or rather tiffin as we called it. I'd already had what we called Chota Hazri at 6 a.m. which was really breakfast. After the meal I'd take an hour for preparation and students could come to ask questions or to discuss essays. At 3 p.m. a cup of tea and then over to college again for another class at 3.30. In the hot weather I usually took a siesta.

The Lutheran Mission Compound was a large one. It was the place where the pioneering work of the Danish and Norwegian Lutherans began. In about 1860 three missionaries came to Benagaria – one was Norwegian, Mr Skrefsrud, and the other two were a Danish couple always known as Papa and Mama Sahib. Their graves are down by the Church they built. The mission grew when the Swedes and Americans became involved. I soon discovered that the real power behind the Church was the Missionaries' Conference. The Lutherans were very unwilling to let go of the purse strings. They had set up the Northern Evangelical Lutheran Church which had its own conference and an appearance of independence, but actually was entirely under the control of the Missionaries' Conference. During the four years I was there it was becoming clear that the day of the missionary was coming to an end. All of us when we went on leave had to get a certificate from the government: "No objection to return". If they thought a missionary was doing a job that an Indian could do, they would refuse to issue the certificate. I remember when the Northern Evangelical Lutheran Church was holding one of their conferences I had three or four missionaries staying as guests in my house. I had noticed that they had an Indian lawyer at the Conference and asked them what he was there for. They replied, "We are working out a constitution for the Church which will mean that the Santals cannot ever alter it." I was shocked at this blatant attempt to control the future and said, "Well, that's easy – they can just all leave your church and start another free from you." They were not very pleased with me and obviously thought I was a bad influence! Afterwards I heard that the lawyer didn't succeed in his task because the Santals had dug their heels in. Johs and Magda Krogh, my colleagues, didn't agree with their mission's policy but felt it was possible to carry on in their own way. I felt that someday the moment of truth would come, and eventually it did.

My four years in Benegaria were very happy ones. As I was teaching in Santali I became proficient in that language. Teaching early Church History in Santali was far from easy especially as I had to explain the various heresies during the first three or four hundred years. The language has no abstract nouns and it was certainly a job to explain abstract concepts in it, but very good for me as I had to really know what I was talking about. Teaching English was also interesting, I had to get them writing essays on various subjects. For instance, in one of the early lessons I chose the subject from a previous LTh English paper: "A visit to a great city". I soon discovered that the students who came from villages had never been to a big city. I suggested to Johs that perhaps we could take them to Calcutta for a few days. We did eventually arrange such a visit and they were amazed. Another subject was about the sea which they had never seen. In my last year we had a visitor from the World Lutheran Federation in Geneva. He asked to come to one of my essay classes. I chose the subject "Communications". We discussed how we communicate with each other – conversation, letters etc. and got onto roads and railways, telegraph and post offices, radio etc. Our visitor was most impressed and said I was teaching concepts. We always needed at least two lessons to discuss an essay theme before there was any chance of getting something written. There were also set books to wrestle with – I remember one called The People of God which I think had been chosen because it was supposed to be "simple English"! There was a chapter on unity which used the example of an orchestra playing. I took my record player to college and played Handel's Largo to the students, but to them it was just a nasty noise! I had to think of something else to express harmony.

Teaching Indian Church History was also interesting. I learnt much in the process. Not least that Thomas the Apostle almost certainly founded the Jacobite Church in Tranquebar (now Kerala).

When I got to the unity debate and the Church of South India, and the discussions about the Church of North India, I was on a sticky wicket because the Lutherans were not interested. The Lutheran students were indignant that they had never heard about it; the subject not having been discussed. The Baptists had heard about it because it had been talked about in their Church meetings. I suggested that the Lutheran students should speak to their Church leaders.

On Sundays Johs, Magda and I often went to Narainpur about six miles away just over the border into Bengal. The Lutherans had a Bengali boarding school there. Ellen Lawson, a Danish missionary, was on the staff and the Headmistress was Neela Das. I used to take their Sunday service for them and enjoyed being able to use my Bengali for a change. In the long hot weather vacation I went back to my old haunts in the Bankura area and spoke at Women's Fellowship meetings. My house in Benagaria was known as Sister Margaret's Holiday Home to my Methodist friends and a number of families and friends came for holidays during my four years there. The children of my friends spoke Bengali and the missionaries' children at Benagaria spoke Santali, but they played together quite happily and had no trouble in communicating over four different languages – English, Norwegian, Santali and Bengali!

The back of my house looked out over the fields to a Muslim village. One day I looked out and saw that the village was on fire. There was a drought at the time, and the wells and tanks were dry. I went over with the Norwegian missionary to see if we could do anything. With us was a young man, a tourist who was cycling across India. There was no water and we just stood with the family and watched the houses burn. Then suddenly the tourist took a bundle of rupee notes from his pocket and pressed them into the hand of the householder. No words were spoken but that money did talk.

After three years teaching, ten of our students sat for the LTh exam. They all passed, four of them with First Class. The folk at

Serampore were delighted as no one had achieved First Class for years. Four of the students went on to Serampore College to study for the BD in English.

In 1968 it was time for me to go home. I had experienced health problems during my four years at Benagaria, culminating in an operation in 1967. I had begun to feel that my time in India was drawing to a close. My parents were ageing and I felt I wouldn't be able to leave them again. However, I went ahead and got my "No objection to return" certificate. I went over to Bengal to say my farewells to all my friends and flew home from Dum Dum airport near Calcutta on March 30th. It was a hundred degrees Fahrenheit in the shade in Calcutta and when I got to Heathrow there was snow on the ground!

With Soila, Romola and Romoni
Barikul, 1955

Chapter 12: Postscript to India

After I left Benagaria the Reverend Ruel Soren, a Santal minister from the Church of Scotland, came for two years to take my place. He, of course, was eventually a presbyter in the Church of North India. While he was there it became clear that the Lutherans did not want to use the men who passed their LTh and had gone on for further training. Ruel used his influence and they were adopted and stationed by the Church of North India. Timotheus Hembrom, who was one of the most brilliant of our students, was rejected by his own church. After getting his BD he went down to Bangalore United Theological College and studied for an MTh. He taught for a while at the Cherapunji Theological College in Assam but for some years now has been the Old Testament Professor at the Bishop's College in Calcutta.

Johs and Magda at last realised that the moment of truth had come and they could no longer stay with their mission. Johs became registrar of Serampore College and both he and Magda taught there until they retired.

All the time I was in India the Reverend Christacharon Pande was Chairman of the Methodist District. He was always known as Sanu Babu to us all. He came of Brahmin stock but Pande is not a Bengali name, so his family must come from further north, possibly Uttar Pradesh. He used to tell the story of his father's conversion to Christianity. Two missionaries had come from Calcutta and were selling scriptures and preaching the Gospel. They angered a Hindu mob and were in danger of being lynched. They took shelter in the door of a house. The door suddenly opened and they were pulled inside. Deprived of their prey the mob soon dispersed. Sanu Babu's father took them in, fed them and put them up for the night. He questioned them and discussed religion with them. In the end they stayed for several days and their host converted to the Christian faith. It was the beginning of the Christian Church in Bankura. His son, Sanu Babu, worked for the YMCA in Calcutta and eventually candidated for the ministry. He became Chairman of the Bengal District in 1948 and remained in the post for over twenty years. He was very greatly loved in the District was a real father-in-God to us all. A man of great stature. His great sorrow was that the union of the Church which he had worked so hard to bring about, came just after he had retired, so he never took office in it.

I remember at Synod in 1951 when he had just returned from his first visit to England. He had been to Oxford for a World Methodist Conference and stayed with my parents who were living in Banbury at the time. He gave my mother a set of Wedgwood fruit dishes which I still have and use. One evening during the Synod he had a group of men friends on his verandah – they were smoking the hookah and passing it around. He was giving them his impressions of England. He told them that he travelled by train from London to Manchester, at that time a four-hour journey. "And do you know", he said, "the compartment was full of people and they didn't speak to each other for the whole journey!" His hearers were amazed and turned to me. "What was the matter with them?" they asked. I replied that English people weren't very talkative on trains. Maybe they thought they wouldn't see their companions again so they didn't bother! "Bapre bap!" they said, "What an opportunity missed! They might have learned something or made some new friends."

Travelling on trains and buses in India was very different. We questioned each other about who we were, where we came from, what did we do, were we married, how many children we had, etc. etc. As I used to spend most of my hot weather holidays in Ootacamund, in the Nilgiri Hills, South India, I spent hours travelling from Calcutta to Madras and back again. You became quite good friends with your travelling companions by the time you had spent nearly two days and two nights on board the Madras Mail!

I have many memories of amusing happenings. Learning a new language was fraught with possibilities for mistakes. The doctor at Sarenga Hospital, Ernest Hollinberg, preached a sermon on "I am the potato of the world". Arlu means potato in Bengali and Arlo means light. A colleague of mine gave a health talk on how diseases were carried by flies and insects. She confused Machi, which means fly, with Mashi, which means maternal aunt, much to the amusement of her audience, who I am sure would never forget her talk.

One night when I was living with John and Joyce Hastings at Denli, we were woken at about 2 a.m. by loud banging on the doors at the back of the house. It turned out to be two or three officials from nearby Raipur. They were checking whether the night-watchman was doing his job. When I called out, "Who's there?", they replied, "Petrol, Memsahib". They meant patrol. We had to sign on the dotted line for them. Another time when a population census was being taken, a group of officials came and set up a table and chairs and interviewed everyone in the village. They wrote the missionary and his wife down correctly, but what was I? I got put down in the column for concubines! Had I been in India for longer I would have told them I was a sister or an aunt. But I had told them I was a paying guest!

When I first became a missionary it never occurred to me that the missionary era was nearly over. But it slowly began to dawn on us that the pattern of our work had to change. In 1954 John Hastings wrote to us all asking us to meet in Sarenga. We spent two days discussing the situation. We had to work ourselves out of a job. The time of the life-long missionary was drawing to a close. The Church in India would have to learn to stand on its own feet and not be dependent on foreign money and personnel. Synod should only ask for new missionaries for special, short-term jobs.

We wrote up what we had discussed and sent it to the Chairman, and a copy to the Missionary Society.

I was lucky because my job in lay training was tailor-made for the situation. The Women's fellowship organisation I set up stood the test of time and has been absorbed into the Church of North India. It has brought women to the fore in all sorts of ways. Romani Garai was one of the women I trained as a Church Worker. She married and joined her husband in a suburb of Calcutta. She had six children, all were Christians and active ones. Before leaving India I visited her family and three or four other Sarenga families whose husbands had jobs in the Post Office. It was a Sunday and I took a service for them. We had planned to have it indoors but so many people wanted to come that we spread mats in the courtyard and about sixty Hindu and Muslim neighbours shared with us. Afterwards the Christian women made tea and we had a great discussion about Christianity. The neighbours were amazed to see a white woman in that area. Now there is a Church of over a hundred members. I talked to two Hindu converts when I visited in 1986 and asked what made them change their religion – they said they lived next door to Romani and her family. "We saw how loving and caring they were to everybody," they said, "and we wanted to be part of that love." Sarenga Church grumbled because they had lost so many members and I pointed out that in so many places Sarenga Christians were spreading the Gospel and founding new churches. The Youth Group at Sarenga Church were also instrumental in founding a Church at Gorbeta which is on the railway line to Bankura. It began in a small way with one or two converts but is now a fully-fledged church where a minister has been appointed.

The Church of North India is much smaller than the Church of South India but it has an influence far greater than its numbers. The Church of South India would like the North to join with them and so have one Church in India. The North is so different from the

South that I'm not sure it would work and the North is afraid of being swamped by the South.

In 1985 I went on a return visit to Bengal with Edna Whewell. We spent time in Calcutta, Sarenga and the Santal Mission, now called the Samedi Pastorate. We had a wonderful reception even though it was seventeen and a half years since I left in 1968. We were received with love and the most wonderful hospitality. Our impression was that the grass-roots church was doing fine. As usual in India there was trouble and lawsuits at the top but that wasn't affecting the growth of the local Churches.

When I went to live in the village of Barikul in 1954, at the request of the Reverend John Hastings, I employed a woman called Mariam Hansda as my cook and cleaner. She had an illegitimate daughter called Nira, whom she wanted to put through school. I had to teach Mariam to cook and make bread and generally look after my house. She had a sister called Santo, who was really a prostitute. They were orphans and had been brought up in the Girls' Hostel in Sarenga. In her teens Mariam had an affair with a Bengali and Nira was the result. She believed he was going to marry her but he had no intention of marrying a casteless tribal woman. Mariam was not an easy person and was generally despised by the people in the village, but she was a good worker and I did my best to make her feel wanted. However, in 1957 she was having another affair with a man in Barikul called Motilal Hembrom. He was a Christian and the village postman. While I was on holiday they were "taken in adultery" and she was driven out of the village. Motilal wanted to marry her but his widowed mother was against it and in fact had organised a group that spied on them and caught them sleeping together. Mariam disappeared out of my life and I couldn't find out where she had gone. Much later on I heard that she was working for a Burmese family in Durgapur steel town. In 1986 just before Edna and I were leaving to go home, I heard that Mariam was in Sarenga – Nira had married into a Bengali family. I went straightaway to see her. She was delighted to see me and was obviously well treated and respected by her son in-law's family. Nira was the mother of six children, three of whom were boys. When I took my leave, Mariam went with me. When we got to the Nurses' Home where Edna and I were staying, Mariam seized my hands, put her arms around me and kissed me – very unusual in India! "I've been waiting years to thank you," she said. "If you hadn't taught me to cook and look after your house, I would never have got the job in Durgapur. That Burmese family were very good to me. I was with them for fourteen years. They helped me get Nira through school and college. Nira worked as a secretary and accountant with a firm in Asansol and the Chakraboti boy met her there. I'm so happy now, I have my home in Asansol and can come here to stay whenever I like. And it's all because of what you did for me."

I felt really overcome by this as I had been rather unwilling to take her on in the beginning. It was a nice way to end my India visit. I was so glad that things worked out so well for her. Until she came to work for me she'd led a miserable life and been very bitter about the way the world had treated her.

When I first arrived in India and went to Sarenga I stayed in the Sisters' bungalow. Florence Smith was packing up to leave Sarenga after a dispute with the Doctor there. The District decided to send her to Bankura as she was in her third term. She got on very well in Bankura and was later posted to Romingang for pastoral work and also to help in the Leprosy Home there. At one time she visited an old lady who was ill and lived alone. Florence was sorry for her and cared for her. She went every day with food, did her washing and prayed with her. There was a young communist, Ramigenj, who had always been very anti-Christian. He noticed that Florence was visiting the old lady and one day he called on her to find out what Florence was up to! "Why does she come?" he asked. "What does she want?" "She loves me," said the old lady. "She looks after me and cares for me. She doesn't demand anything." "But why does she do it?", he asked. "She's not your relative." "She does it because she loves the Lord Jesus." The young man called on Florence to see what this was all about. The result was that in the end he became a Christian and worked as a Christian social worker in a village near Sarenga.

Reverend Christa Charon Pande
Chairman, Bengal District

Chapter 13: Reflections

As I look back to 1947 when I sailed for China, it seems like another world. Talk about Abraham not knowing "whither he went", I certainly didn't know what we were approaching in China. There were five of us young Methodist missionaries who were all to be out of China in two or three years. It seemed like a tragedy when I had to leave China in 1949, but it wasn't. Once in India I realised that my China experience was of infinite value. For one thing it meant I didn't only have England to compare India with. I also had China and that made a lot of difference. Also, because of what I had learned in China I soon knew what God wanted me to do in India. So I resisted Synod's efforts to place me in institutions like Bankura Christian College or one of the schools. I knew my task was in lay training. I was led later into ministerial training, but it was all of a piece.

Unlike South India the North had nothing like the Mass Movements. Hinduism and Islam were stronger in the North and it was much harder to convert people. In my early days in the Santal Mission there was a hard-line Hindu group, the Hindu Seva Sangha, who were anti-Christian, but they didn't last long and I never personally faced any opposition. Indeed, all the people were very friendly and ready to talk religion. Every February there was a Mela (a fair) in a village called Matgoda. Traders came from far and wide and set up shops made of straw and bamboo and thousands of people came to buy. In John Hastings' time, the Church set up a Gospel shop and we sold hundreds of Bible portions and Christian books. I used to take a group of women who wanted to take part. The men slept in the shop, but the women went every evening to a nearby village, where there were Christian families. During the year in the course of our wanderings, we often met up with people who had bought books and asked us questions about them. During the time I was in the Circuit there were a few conversions and I was present at a number of public baptisms in rivers and tanks.

Originally the local primary schools in the villages had been founded by the Church. In my time the government had taken them over but in many of them the teachers were still Christians. Most of the teachers, Christian or otherwise, had been trained in the Mission College at Sarenga. In both China and India, it was the Church that pioneered educational and medical work, and I imagine the same was true elsewhere. Leprosy work was also pioneered by the Churches. During my time Indian workers were gradually taking responsibility for the work, and institutions like Ludhiana and Vellore had trained the first doctors. Indian universities like Calcutta, Delhi and Madras also established their own medical schools. Indian doctors were going abroad for further training too. Things were changing fast.

After I had been home for seventeen and a half years I went back to India for a two-month visit. Of course, since I left, the Church of North India had come into being. There is a bishop in Durgapur diocese now. I fear that at the "top" things were not going very smoothly, but we felt very encouraged by the grass roots activities both in Sarenga and the Santal Mission Circuits. While we were in Calcutta we went to the cathedral for a carol competition. The Bishop of Calcutta was the Right Reverend Dinesh Gorai and he had just finished a term as Moderator of the Church of North India. All the churches in the Calcutta area had been asked to compose a new Bengali Carol, words and music, and everyone was competing. It was marvellous what they had achieved. Dinesh was a Sarenga boy, his father was the pharmacist at the hospital there. He has been a really good bishop and done a lot for the Church.

The Church in China has had a rough passage. Since 1911 the country had been in political turmoil, what with warlords and Civil War. Protestant missions only started in China after the Opium War so they had been working barely a century when communism came along. In 1949, the year I left, it was reckoned there were about 750,000 Protestant Christians – not many in a country which then had a population of 450 million or so. For nearly thirty years I heard absolutely nothing about the Chinese Church. The few visitors who got into China reported that the Churches had closed and were being used in different ways. But remembering the enthusiasm and determination of the Christians in East China I always believed something would survive. In 1976 I attended a Central Committee meeting of the Methodist Missionary Society – the Reverend Bob Whyte was one of the speakers and he reported news of Christians in Zhejiang Province where Ningpo is. I made myself known to him and joined the China Study Project on the spot! After that more and more news began to come out. The Cultural Revolution was over and Churches were being given back. I got to know about old friends in China and began to correspond with them. This culminated in a visit to China, with a Friends of the Church in China party, in May 1987. We combined sightseeing with visiting churches in Beijing, Shanghai, Chunking, Nanjing, Chengdu – but my main joy was when, with a friend, we found our way to Ningpo via Hanzhou. It was wonderful to find so many old friends still around after forty years. The Reverend Francis Fan had been a young minister at our main church in Ningpo city when I left in 1949. He was banished to the country for several years, "pushing buffaloes" as he described it. He was then in prison in solitary confinement for two years. He said his wife had a very tough time bringing up their five children on very little income. He told me he had a blacked-out window in his cell. He found a pebble on the floor and with it scratched two Hebrew words on the window – Ebenezer ("Hitherto hath the Lord helped me") and Jehovah-Jireh ("The Lord will provide"). When he felt down he would run his fingers over them and pray. He would recite Bible passages in his cell. We heard many stories like that on our travels.

We did not gain the impression of the House Church movement being against the Three Self Church. In the Ningpo area they seemed to work together. We were told that "House Church" wasn't really a correct description as the groups were so large they mainly met in the open air. The Ningpo Church provided preachers and worship leaders for the House Churches. At all the Churches we visited and worshipped in, the congregation largely had their own Bibles. The Amity Press in Nanjing has printed several million Bibles, and continues to do so. When I was in Ningpo between 1947 and 1949 the Church there was already well able to look after itself. They were glad to have missionaries' help, but it was not a mortal blow when we had to leave. And through the war and the Japanese Occupation they had managed without financial help from abroad.

On the last night of our visit to China, Margaret James and I were in a hotel in Hanzhou. Mr and Mrs Fan came to say goodbye, bringing with them three girl theological students, all from Ningpo. Mr Fan was then principal of the Hanzhou Theological College. We had a wonderful evening with them. In answer to a question from Margaret James the three girls shared their testimony with us. They had all converted to Christianity during the Cultural Revolution, when religion was forbidden. One was a member of a Christian family who had secretly kept the faith. The other two had communist parents, had never been to Church or heard of Christianity. They started asking questions about the meaning of life in their teens. Each found a Christian friend who lent them a Bible. As soon as the Churches reopened they were there and asking to be prepared for baptism. We realised why the Church had grown, in spite of persecution. We heard stories like this in all the places we visited. From 750,000 in 1949 the Protestant Church is now several million strong and growing fast. Its age range is from young, through middle-age to old. A miracle indeed!

The Indian Church was still very missionary-ridden in 1949. They had never had to manage on their own like the Chinese Church. Fortunately, most missionaries realised the writing was on the wall – before the home boards and societies realised it. During the 1960s the Indian government decided to cut down on missionaries by introducing new visas stamped with "No Objection to Return". When we went on leave we had to apply for this visa. If they thought we were doing a job an Indian could do, they would refuse the visa. This had a very rapid effect on the number of missionaries allowed in. If you stayed home too long, the "No Objection" lapsed and you had to apply again. When I left India in 1968 I had "No Objection to Return", but I stayed home until my parents died in 1971, by which time I couldn't have renewed my visa.

I am very thankful for several things in my pilgrimage. I'm glad I decided to study History at University. I think it gave me a very balanced view of events and people. I'm glad to I went to China first and India afterwards, so that I had two standards of judgement. Living in two foreign countries influenced my ideas about my own country. My parents used to accuse me of not being patriotic. I remember having an argument with my father about the events in Suez in 1956. He thought what we did was all right, but I remembered India's anger about it. Somebody quite recently said to me, "I think the Chinese make too much fuss about the Opium Wars." He's a Local Preacher as well! But I lived in one of the Treaty Ports and know how humiliated the Chinese still feel about the way they were treated. Coming back to this country was very hard – the waste of food, racism, effortless British superiority. All these things offended me. Working in the Queen's College, Birmingham for three years helped me through and also studying for the Diploma of Pastoral Studies at Birmingham University.

The other day I watched the service from Westminster Abbey to celebrate the Queen and Prince Philip's Golden Wedding and celebrated my own fifty years' anniversary of embarking for China on that very day. It started me reminiscing about my life. I feel very proud to have been a part of the Church life in China and India. I think we have a lot to learn from both Churches. It's easy for us to criticise them, but they have their own way of dealing with things that have gone wrong. They need our prayers and support.

As I approach the end of my life, I look back and realise that God has been with me every step of the way. There have been times of disappointment and failure, but my overwhelming impression is of being guided from one thing to another. I've always been shown what I must do next. Even now at seventy-six years old, I realise there is more ahead. To quote the Reverend Francis B James, "God can make these later stages of the journey as rich an adventure as any that went before. If the zest of the beginning is gone, there may come in its place the sense of fulfilment and the anticipation of the end."

Jesus I fain would find
By zeal for God in me,
Thy yearning pity for mankind,
Thy burning charity.

In me thy spirit dwell;
In me thy mercies move
So shall the fervour of my zeal
Be the pure flame of love.

Amen!

Chapter 14: Ningbo Revisited

A postscript to the "Friends of the Church in China" tour: May-June 1987

After a rather traumatic journey from Xiamen, via Shanghai, my great friend, Margaret James, and I eventually arrived at Hangzhou at about 9:30 a.m. on Friday, May 29th. The Reverend Francis Fan was there to meet us. We booked the train to Ningbo the following morning and then he took us to the seminary in Jie Fang road. They use the old American Presbyterian Church, which is not the most convenient building; students have to eat their meals at their desks in the classroom. After a wash and a change in the guest room, we were taken on a tour of inspection. In the Church there were five or six harmoniums tucked away in various parts of the building and several students practising hard! Part of their training is to learn to play them. We also noticed a number of students sitting or kneeling in prayer and others studying. We were introduced to the students and both Margaret and I had to say a few words.

The church reopened for worship in 1979. They had to go around searching for all their furnishings, which had disappeared during the Cultural Revolution. As in Chengdu they got most of it back. Mrs Fan gave us a meal of fried noodles and fresh pineapple. At this point the Amity Foundation Methodist arrived: Rosemary Brookes. We all sat and looked at my old photographs taken in Ningbo so long ago. Mrs Fan wept when she saw the photo of herself with her husband and their two youngest children, which they had given me at Christmas in 1948. Mr Fan explained that they had lost everything when the red guards came: photos, books, Bibles and all their possessions were thrown out and burned. He was banished to the country and forced to work in the fields. He said that as he pushed the buffaloes along, he would sing hymns, pray and recite the Bible to himself. The 23rd Psalm meant a tremendous lot. He managed to hide one small Bible on the top of a pillar in his mother's house. Needless to say I returned the little family photograph to them, as I could see Mrs Fan wanted it badly. She shed quite a few tears as we looked at the old photos and, while we did, Mr Fan chatted away about the horror of the Cultural Revolution. Then he spoke of his grandfather, who became a Christian in Shih Pu, a fishing port to the south of Ningbo. He was a powerful preacher and helped to found the church there. He told us that the old man went on preaching up to the day of his death. Just before he died he preached his heart out at an evangelistic meeting where many were converted by his words. He then crept up the stairs and died in his sleep. His son, Mr Fan's father also became a minister and wanted one of his sons to follow in his footsteps. It was Mr Fan's father who was a close friend of the Reverend Harold Tomlinson (a former Methodist missionary) and took him around as he travelled the circuit and taught him the Ningbo dialect. Francis became a minister like his father and trained at the Jinling seminary at Nanjing. He was a brilliant student and had just won a scholarship to study in the States when the Japanese invasion stopped him going. He told us he had had another chance to go in 1949 but was afraid he wouldn't be able to return to China if he went.

After this session Rosemary took us to our hotel. Mr Fan was busy for the rest of the day and said he would see us on our return from Ningbo. We were quite tired and only too glad to relax. We spent the evening with Rosemary and it was very interesting to hear of her experiences. She has signed on for another year.

On Saturday, May 30th we caught the 8 a.m. train to Ningbo. We were both feeling extremely tired and hadn't been able to get any breakfast. We were revived by the green tea provided and some digestive biscuits. At the station we were met by three friends: the

Reverend Dzang Tseh Feng, whom I remembered as a youngish Methodist minister in 1949, now aged 74 and retired; the Reverend Shu Shing Yuan, a candidate for the ministry in 1949 and a probationer in the country area of Wang Chi, now the same age as me, sixty-six, and the secretary of the Ningbo Three Self committee; and Mr Wu Shin Pay an ex-Baptist who was business manager of the American Baptist Hwa Mei hospital (now Ningbo number two hospital). They held a banner on high saying "welcome Miss Budd and Miss James!" We were made to feel very welcome. These three looked after us like members of their own family all the time we were there. They had brought a minibus from the Friendship store, where Mr Dzang's nephew worked and he too was most helpful. They had booked us into the Ningbo hotel which we found cheap, friendly and comfortable. When we were washed and fed they took us to a reception room on the third floor and we sat and chatted freely over tea. I asked about various people and churches and they were surprised that I remembered so much. Nearly all the village churches I remembered are going strong as is the Ningbo church since they have pastors and lay leaders to help them. The Hangzhou seminary is one of the regional ones designated to train pastors in the rural areas. They hope that before long each main village church and meeting point will have their own pastor. In Ningbo itself at present they are only using the ex-Anglican Centennial church, which was the newest building, but they are to get back three or more very soon. Poh Dong, the old Methodist north bank church, now a factory, is to be given back and used for worship. It was interesting to see what a building looked like before it is handed back. A mess! The inside will have to be completely refurbished as all the fittings are gone. Kae Ming, which was the main Methodist church before the revolution is also coming back. It's been used as a 'Children's Palace' and is in good condition but no inside furnishings at all. We were told that it would be used for children's work. The other church to come back is an ex-Assemblies of God Church on the east bank. This is to cater for the many Christians on that side of the city. In 1949 they used a converted house church but in 1966 it went back to residential use.

They have three services every Sunday at Centennial Church and we were told that a thousand to fifteen hundred people attend each service: at 8:30 a.m. 2:30 p.m. and 8 p.m. We were asked a great many questions about previous missionaries and they told us about some of the things they did. Then they talked about plans for the next two days. What did we want to do? It was all very free and easy. We said we wanted to go to church the next morning and they said they would come and fetch us and that there would be a small reception after the service. Would I like a trip around the city in the afternoon to see all the old places? And what about Monday? I asked if it was possible to go out into the country. There seemed to be no problem: we could get where we liked, time was the only limitation. During my two years in Ningbo, a senior colleague, Doris Coombs, often took me with her on her preaching expeditions at the weekends. I remembered going with her to Qinghai at the mouth of the river Uong, ten miles or so from Ningbo. So I asked to go there. They then departed and we were gratefully left to ourselves for the rest of the day.

Next morning Messrs. Dzang, Shu and Wu took us to church. Like everywhere else we'd been, the building was crowded to the doors and more. There were certainly well over a thousand people gathered for worship. Very efficient lady ushers with attractive badges seized us and piloted us up into the gallery. Our friends sat with us. They were practising a hymn which turned out to be "Jesu you lover of my soul" to the American tune. Mr Shu's son-in-law was teaching them. He had a very nice baritone voice. At the piano was a retired ex-primary school headmistress, who transferred to the organ when the service started and someone else took over on the piano. At 8.30 prompt the robed choir filed in (such things were not seen forty years ago!) and opened the service with an introit from the new hymn book. The service was led by pastor Zah (quite young - forty-ish) and the sermon preached by Pastor Kan (ex -

Assemblies of God - sixty-ish) The sermon lasted for fifty minutes, so they haven't changed! There was a good deal of congregational participation: Psalm 1 was recited all together before the first prayer, punctuated by amens and praises just like it used to be. During the sermon, whenever Pastor Kan quoted the Bible, which was pretty often, he usually got the people to say it with him. He gave them time to find the place and the ushers helped in this. The choir sang an anthem, again from the new book about Jesus knocking at the door. The sermon was thoroughly biblical, relating our faith to Christian living. They then sang a hymn: "I know in whom I have believed". Then the pastor said, "let us pray." And we went suddenly praying all together: the pastor starting and everybody saying their own prayer out loud. I remembered this so well: it got louder and louder for five or six minutes; "storming the gates of heaven!" Then they sang the chorus of the last hymn and said the Lord's prayer. After that Pastor Sung (elderly ex-Anglican) led intercessions and pastor Zah said the benediction. This was the most prayerful service we attended in China. Afterwards, the gallery was cleared and the table and chairs set up with the inevitable green tea and Chinese coke. I met a number of old friends and it was wonderful to see them again. We heard that: over a thousand new Christians had been baptised since 1979, they have seven theological students studying for the Ministry, six girls at Hangzhou, and one boy who has completed two years at Hangzhou and gone on to Nanjing. These are fully supported by the Ningbo church.

We were told that services were also held during the week and that a weekly Bible class was held every Wednesday at Mr Shu's home. There are also choir practices and classes for enquirers and preparation for baptism.

In the afternoon our three friends collected us in the minibus and I was taken on a trip down memory lane. Much of Ningbo is quite recognisable and even after forty years some of the streets were almost unchanged, but there has been tremendous development, especially on the outskirts of the city. They are obviously hoping to attract many tourists and another big hotel was being built just opposite to ours and others are planned. They have their own friendship store. Certainly Ningbo is well worth a visit; a bit like Suzhou with all its waterways and rivers. But the river Uong is looking very much more built up and there are more dock areas and large ships coming in. The old foreign graveyard with its memorials to pioneer missionaries and their families and British soldiers who died fighting the Tai Pings under Chinese Gordon has gone. But our old compound is still there, including the houses and the ginkgo tree, but all very overgrown now. The army was occupying the houses but they were very friendly and allowed us to have a look. Our friends told us that on all the mission land, including this compound, the church had a prior claim, and that they could ask for it back if they had a good reason for wanting it.

Next door was the old fifth primary school with additional new buildings; now of course a government school but obviously flourishing. Although it was a Sunday, all the children and teachers were there preparing for international children's day on June 1st. There was a festive air and the children were busy making decorations and pinning up paintings. The teachers were extremely friendly and asked us to sit down and drink tea. They said, "you all know Mrs Dzing who used to be on the staff here." They sent for her. She lives close by and she soon came carrying one of her grandchildren. I recognised her at once. Her brother was the Reverend Dzing Sing-Ming who was chairman of the district when I first arrived. He became very ill with tuberculosis and died in 1951. She recognised me as well and remarked that I was a lot bigger than I used to be! I was pleased to think that these institutions funded by the church were still serving the community. The two Christian high schools, Chitong School for boys and Uong Kong School for girls, are still going strong. We looked at the old North Bank Church and also Kae Ming which I mentioned earlier and also went along to the east bank where I used to play the harmonium.

Here a moving thing happened. An ordinary church member recognised me out of the blue! He didn't know I was around. "I know her." He exclaimed, "that's Bah Mai-ga who used to play our hymns for us!" He turned out to be someone I remembered, as he was converted when I was there.

There used to be only one pontoon bridge across the main river, the Bridge of boats we called it, and one proper bridge across the second of the three rivers on which Ningbo is built. Now there are three pukka bridges and the pontoon bridge has been moved upstream for pedestrians only.

In the evening Dr Samuel Wu came to visit us. In our day the Wus were a well-to-do educated Christian family, most of whom had studied in America. Samuel was a doctor and with his wife ran a private clinic and hospital next door to our compound. It was called Tien Seng hospital and Samuel was a very good doctor to us. His sister Lily, the oldest of the family, was married to the Reverend Marcus Chan, a member of the China Christian Council. She was living at home in 1947, as her husband was abroad, and she was my first Chinese teacher. I heard afterwards from Mr Fan a little of Dr Wu's story. After Liberation he was forced to close his clinic and hand over equipment to the government. He was then made the medical superintendent of the Hwa Mei hospital (founded by the American Baptist Mission) now the Ningbo number 2 hospital. The official guidebook for the city says that it was founded by a Christian mission in the 1920s. When the Cultural Revolution came along he was demoted and sent to clean the streets of Ningbo, dragging a dustcart around. After having a terrible time for several years he was reinstated and became the deputy health officer for Ningbo. He is now retired and not very well. I was pleased to see him again though his visit was only a short one. He was very friendly and gave me family news, but he was on his way to the 8 p.m. service at the church so could not stay long.

On Monday, June 1st we were taken to Qinghai. It was pouring with rain and on the way we could see nothing. Gone were the days

106

of the little river steamers, there is now a railway and a good motor road all the way, so we went in the minibus. (We spent quite a lot of money on the minibus but felt it was worth it, not only to see as much as we could but also because we realised how much our Chinese friends were enjoying themselves on these outings) Qinghai is now being developed as a major port and as we drove into what is now a town, I realised at once that its rural character is no more. On the roadside waiting for us was Pastor Yeh Tsei-feng who took us to the church. And there was the little chapel just as I remembered it! The cross over one door and the characters "Qi-toh Dong" Christian Church carved on it. As soon as we went in we realised what a welcome was afoot and that a meal was being cooked. We looked at the old chapel with its bamboo seats and remembered old times. Then we were seated for tea and refreshments. As well as our three friends and Pastor Yeh, there was another lay leader and also a young woman worker, Miss Wu Tzu-yiah, who has just graduated from the Hangzhou seminary and is now a probationary pastor in the Qinghai area. There were also two Christian ladies doing the cooking but who kept coming and joining in the conversation. This was a very valuable session, as we were completely private and everyone talked freely. After talking about missionaries, who had spent a lot of the time in Qinghai and the surrounding villages, and asking about people I remembered, we learned about the church. They have a membership now of over seven hundred with new enquirers coming all the time. They have two services every Sunday, five hundred or so people attend each service. Many Christians coming from the villages bring food to cook on the premises, staying most of the day for prayer and Bible study. I asked about village churches that I had visited with Doris Coombs. All of them are flourishing, with increasing numbers of Christians. The villages nearer the town use Qinghai as their meeting point, but one of the villages, Lod Do Gyiao (Ningbo spelling!) has built their own church and numbers are growing rapidly. They also said that preachers and pastors are sent out twice a month from Ningbo to go around the villages to teach, preach and take communion services etc. "we try to keep up the Methodist tradition," they said. We talked also about the other "circuits" in the old Methodist district and what was happening to the village churches there. Tsing Yi, where a new church building was opened in 1949 has its church building back and is now a meeting point for a wide area. They hope that one of their students, now in training at Hangzhou will be appointed to work there. As there is now a motor road all the way to Tsing Yi, helpers us are now going out as frequently as they can manage. Most of the churches I remembered in the Xiang San and Shih Pu circuits are still going strong; Xiang San is the biggest, but Shih Pu comes a close second. Ds Ts, a little church built on a rocky hill which always did serve a wide area is bigger than ever and is crowded with young people. Kyiah Kyi, a lovely little walled fishing town, also has a growing membership. Some of the smaller ones too, like Tseng Tiao on the Nimrod Sound, are meeting points for a wide area.

The subject also came up regarding the unequal treaties and the treaty ports, of which Ningbo was one. Christians had suffered a lot of criticism over this, as missionaries had entered China through these ports after the Opium War. They realised that most missionaries were unhappy about this association. On the other hand, how could they have allowed the Chinese to get things like opium through these ports? They are glad now that the Gospel came in as well as opium. Through the Three Self movement the stigma of Christian foreignness has gone.

By this time the rain had cleared and we went to have a look at the town. We were taken to a small charming little port, as nice as anything we had seen on the tour, with a lake and flowers and a really splendid playground with lots of interesting things for the children to do. International Children's Day is a school holiday and whole families were there with their children. After an enormous feast at the church, cooked by the two Christian ladies in an incredibly inconvenient kitchen, we were taken, at my request, to what used to be a coastal headland. It is a hill with a small Buddhist temple at the top with a garden. We climbed the steps carved from the rock; several hundred I should think. The temple had been vandalised by the red guard and is now being repaired for the monks who have returned. The gardens have been tidied up and replanted and are absolutely beautiful. The view from the top of the mountains and the river and sea are lovely. But to my amazement the hill is no longer just above the beach as there has been land reclamation going on and the shore is now quite a distance away. We could see an enormous dockland development going on where the river Uong meets the sea. In the distance we could see some of the islands of the Chusan Archipelago. Inland there was a vista of mountains and we could see the boats and ships sailing up and down the river. The river is navigable for sizeable ships right up to Ningbo. Altogether a most interesting and enjoyable day, enlivened by the obvious enjoyment of our Chinese friends, who were revelling in being together and able to talk to us and to each other. We learned so much about them and the church in China just by our conversation as we went along.

The next morning, we were taken to the station to catch our train to Hangzhou and sadly said farewell to our three friends, who had been so good to us. We had given them a few small gifts the previous night and before we left they gave us something too. The best was a Hangzhou silk woven picture of the Ascension. They were woven in one of the government silk weaving factories in Hangzhou, but not sold publicly because of the Christian subject. Mr Fan told us later that a Christian widow had bought up a lot to give to the Christians in Ningbo. We shall treasure them. They also gave us a book of sermons in Chinese; these are published two or three times a year. Mr Dzang and Mr Fan have sermons in this one.

Our train journey was memorable because it was one of the few clear sunny days we had. The mountains were showing and the countryside looked beautiful. We couldn't stop taking photographs. Mr Fan met us again and this time took us to the hotel in the college minibus. He told us he would be back at 3 p.m. to take us out on the West lake. He took us the 'peoples' way'; no private boat for us. We boarded crowded steamers which hopped from island to island. We visited three in all and like our friends in Ningbo, Mr Fan was enjoying himself as much as we were. As we went we talked, and it was crushed on crowded boats that I heard some sad stories of what had happened to a number of the people I used to know.

Our last evening was one of the highlights of the whole tour. Mr and Mrs Fan came to our hotel and brought with them three women students from Ningbo, who were studying at his seminary. We took them up to our room and had an absolutely wonderful evening of fellowship with them. The three girls asked many questions about the Church in England. Had we plenty of young people? Did we have women ministers? What about the churches working together? etc. etc. Then Margaret James asked the girls about their families and what they thought of them becoming pastors in the church. In response to this the three of them in turn gave us their testimony; it was quite unexpected and very moving.

Miss Dzang To-ing aged twenty-five was the first to answer. She said she was a convert and the first one to become a Christian in her family. While she was still at school she began to feel uneasy. She wanted to be good and to help her country and community but couldn't find herself. This worried her a lot and then she met a young Christian, who told her about Jesus. He took her to church; by this time the churches had reopened. She became very interested and kept on going. Finally, she prayed to Jesus, confessed her sins and felt she was forgiven. She entered a class to prepare for baptism and became a believer. At first her family were not very pleased, especially her father. But three months after her conversion, her mother came to church and then her younger sister and her grandmother. They are all now baptised Christians. She dedicated herself to the will of God and then began to feel she was called to the ministry. She prayed about this for nearly three years before she finally offered, was accepted and went to the seminary. Her father tried to forbid her to go to college, but now is much more sympathetic.

Miss Mai Tse-yu, aged thirty-one, was the next to speak. She came from a Christian family, who had stuck to their faith through the hardships of the Cultural Revolution. She came to know Jesus for herself when she was twenty years old. She gave her heart to God and dedicated her life to him. At that time, she was working in a cotton mill, but began to feel that God had something else for her to do. She saw the need of the growing church and realised that their beloved ageing leaders were not going to live forever. She saw something she could do for God and the church and so she offered herself. She felt great happiness and peace in being in Christ and doing God's will.

Miss Dzang, aged twenty-eight, said that she came from a non-Christian family. She grew up during the Cultural Revolution when religion was banned. She was in her late teens at school when she began to wonder about the meaning of life. Who are we? Where are we going? What are we here for? And then by chance she met a friend who was a Christian and she began to hear about the gospel. Then she had the chance to read a Bible. (I asked her, "how did you manage to get hold of a Bible at that time?") She replied that her Christian friend had hidden one and let her borrow it (which must have been a very risky thing to do). She knelt down and prayed to God. "God heard me," she said. "Christ spoke to me." She offered herself to him and was converted. "The spirit was moving me," she said. Then Mr Fan said, "yes, and on the very first Sunday in January 1979, when the church reopened, she was there."

We then had a time of prayer together and began to say our farewells. Gifts were exchanged and at that moment Rosemary Brookes arrived. I think if she had come earlier we might not have heard those testimonies. By this time we felt we knew each other so well, it was hard to see them go. The Fans gave me a beautiful dress length of green silk. I was quite overwhelmed by their generosity. They also had a present for Margaret. Fortunately, we had already decided to give Mrs Fan an Indian sari that Margaret had brought with her. It wasn't new but was a very pretty one and she was delighted with it. We gave Mr Fan some books of prayers and other bits and pieces for the seminary and also had enough of our booklets left to give to the three girls. I don't suppose I shall ever see them again but we shall never forget them. All the time, on this part of the tour in particular, I felt I was a representative of those who had gone before me: the Coombs, Jack Gedye, Slaters, Tomlinson's, Conybeares, Bates, Sheppards and so many others who helped to sow the seed and plant the church. I just want to join with those dear ladies at Qinghai, raise my hands and say, "shi shi Jesu!" Thank you Jesus!

Lightning Source UK Ltd.
Milton Keynes UK
UKHW010211271118
332995UK00015B/1965/P